D0845518

Apartment interiors

Boca Raton Public Library, Boca Raton, FL

APARTMENT INTERIORS
Edition 2007

Author: Carles Broto
Publisher: Carles Broto
Editorial Coordinator: Jacobo Krauel
Graphic designer & production: Dimitri Kottas, Pilar Chueca
Text: contributed by the architects, edited and translated by
William George, Marta Rojals and Judy Thomson

© Carles Broto i Comerma
Jonqueres, 10, 1-5, Barcelona 08003, Spain
Tel.: +34 93 301 21 99
Fax: +34-93-301 00 21
info@linksbooks.net
www. linksbooks.net

All rights reserved. No part of this book may be used or reproduced in
any manner whatsoever without written permission except in the case
of brief quotations embodied in critical articles and reviews.

Apartment interiors

index

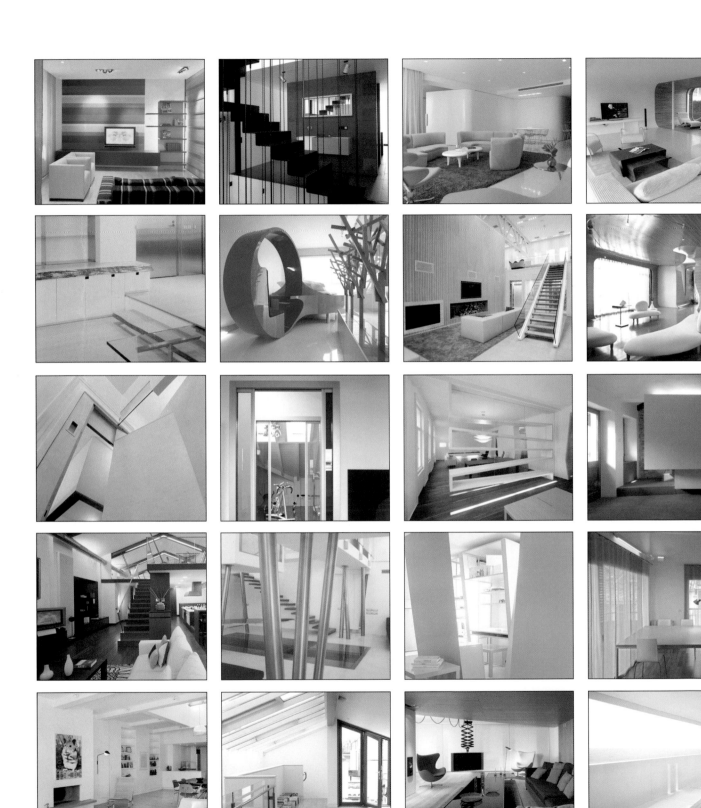

introduction

The dwelling is the warm and pleasant refuge in which we feel protected, our place of rest and work, the scenario in which our daily life is enacted, the space in which the essence of each biography is best revealed, a place of encounter and confrontation in which we spend most of our time.

Interior design is currently one of the most innovative disciplines of architecture. Contemporary architects are aware that there is a need for multi-functional and polyvalent spaces and at the same time highly defined spaces that are pleasant and calm and make their inhabitants feel comfortable. They attempt to meet the needs of the 21st century through the interplay of interior and exterior and the integration with the surroundings. Two basic elements in their work are the combination of materials such as wood, glass and steel, and the bold use of open spaces with hardly any divisions, in which light becomes a basic element of the deign.

The search for bold and completely original forms that are adapted to the lifestyle of their inhabitants is often another factor that leads to experimentation and creativity with forms and materials.

This volume presents a wide range of proposals and styles that show the tendencies and ideas of a new interior architecture in which there seems to be no place for unnecessary decorative concessions, and the challenge focuses on creating a space as a sanctuary in which to take refuge from chaos.

Filippo Bombace

Coliseum views

This small apartment in Rome is right opposite the Coliseum. Its location sparked off a debate between the young family who were going to live there and the architect due to renovate it. The family favored a classical interior, while the architect saw the project as a unique opportunity to reflect on the incomparable view of a major part of Rome's architectural heritage by using open, innovative design ideas. They finally agreed to structure the space into what, above all else, should be a home, but at the same time to decorate and enrich it by handling the spaces carefully and using a contemporary color scheme.

A tunnel of fabrics, set up on a framework of sliding curtains, streamlines the way in to the new layout of the daytime area. The range of colors is evocative of the neighborhood flavors, textures and history, as well as the verdant Celio gardens which are nearby, and it outlines the distribution of the project. A faded antique green, the subtle grey tones of Roman stones, the beige of the travertine and cardinal purple are echoed partly in the fabric coverings and upholstery and partly in the large mural which defines the television wall. This mural is aligned with the bookshelves and a stone panel, marked by horizontal streaks of basalt. A blue fluorescent light is embedded behind the panel.

This color scheme continues through into the dining area where there is a striking apple green table. The open-plan kitchen gives directly on to the living room although it has its own separate space reached from a corridor-cum-larder. It has a linear work surface including the hob and overhead cupboards, which contrast with the small low breakfast bar.

Both bathrooms can be reached from the corridor which leads to the bedrooms, through sliding doors. This series of doors, which reproduce the basic colors of the whole scheme, gives character to the corridor which leads to the sleeping area.

So as not to interrupt the lively flow of color between corridor and living room, the two bathrooms are decorated in monochromatic tones using industrial Ardesia stone. The only distinguishing feature is a block of color on the wall: apple green in his bathroom and mauve in hers.

The same color scheme is repeated in the bedrooms as well (alternating apple green and mauve) while different shades of grey lend color to the master bedroom. In this room the bed slots in below a small mezzanine which acts as an essential lookout point for visitors to see the famous panorama. It also leads to the tiny but poetic study area set up on the same level.

The overall atmosphere is completed with a bleached oak floor covering, the carefully designed play of halogen and fluorescent lighting and the whole geometric feel which, combined with the recurring color scheme, brings the space together into a dynamic whole.

Location:
Rome, Italy
Collaborator:
Valentina Brindisi
Photographs:
Luigi Filetici

They finally agreed to structure the space into what above all else should be a home, but at the same time to decorate and enrich it by handling the spaces carefully and using a contemporary color scheme.

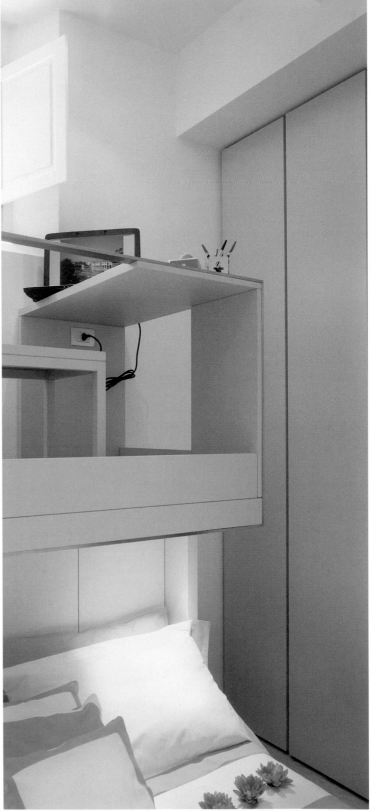

A faded antique green, the subtle grey tones of Roman stones, the beige of the travertine and cardinal purple are echoed partly in the fabric coverings and upholstery (the Mussi sofa is covered with a Kvadrat fabric, as are the dining chairs) and partly in the large mural (based on a drawing by the architect) which defines the television wall.

Slade Architecture

Apartment in Miami Beach

This apartment in South Beach, Miami was designed for a young couple as a very "Miami" vacation home. Only occupied temporarily by the client and occasional guests, the renovation aimed to maximize the ocean views and open, informal atmosphere while being flexible enough to retain privacy.

In the original layout two bedrooms were separated from the living room by sheetrock walls coming off the continuous curtain wall so the expansive view was cut into three. The primary objective was to free the whole width of the curtain wall so all the windows could be seen at once, using materials and colors that suggest a continuation of the interior into the exterior.

To achieve this openness and yet retain the bedrooms, two transformable "walls" were designed, a moving wall unit and a pivot wall. They provide a dynamic, flexible way of configuring the space so the bedrooms can be incorporated into the main living space, creating a much bigger area, and the windows and views are shared between spaces. The guest room has a combination storage closet and wall which hangs from the ceiling and slides out from the demising wall to create a bedroom. When folded and closed the space becomes part of the living area. Operated by a removable crank-driven mechanism the wall incorporates drawers, a hanging space and the door to the bedroom and can conceal the Murphy Bed mounted on the demising wall.

A 10 foot wide full-height pivoting wall was created for the master bedroom which opens so the window can be seen from the living area while protecting the bedroom's privacy.

Corners were rounded off to create a continuous flowing surface that starts in the entry and ends in this operable pivot wall, accentuating the depth of the apartment.

The bed and the cantilevered desk in the master bedroom were designed in 3D on the computer, then manufactured from solid blocks of foam reinforced with steel and aluminum and covered in a lacquer finished, fiberglass skin. This finish is reminiscent of a surfboard, in keeping with the environment and the client's personal interest in surfing. The desk is anchored to a floor-to-ceiling steel column embedded in the millwork. The bed shape came by lofting a flower shaped base with a rectangular bed. The underside and shape of this bed are important because they are reflected in the glossy resin floor. It is a loose piece of furniture that sits on the floor. The finish materials were carefully chosen to accentuate the view and internalize the ocean, sky and sand: the blue custom Resin floor has a sand-like texture with a smooth surface while the translucent curtains enhance the blue and the glossy white walls reflect the ocean. The interior view, with its rosewood paneling and warmer colors, emphasizes solidity in contrast with the bright finishes on the ocean side.

Location:
Miami, Florida, USA
General Contractor:
Edward Nieto Design Group
Moving wall unit fabricator:
Jesus Tejedor
Stereo A/V:
Red Rose (NY)/ Interseckt (Miami)
Fiberglass desk and Bed:
Slade Architecture (Design) and Tom McGuire (Fabrication)
Resin Floors:
Fusion Floors
Curtains:
Deco Center
Furnishings:
Slade Architecture
Photographs:
Ken Hayden / Redcover.com

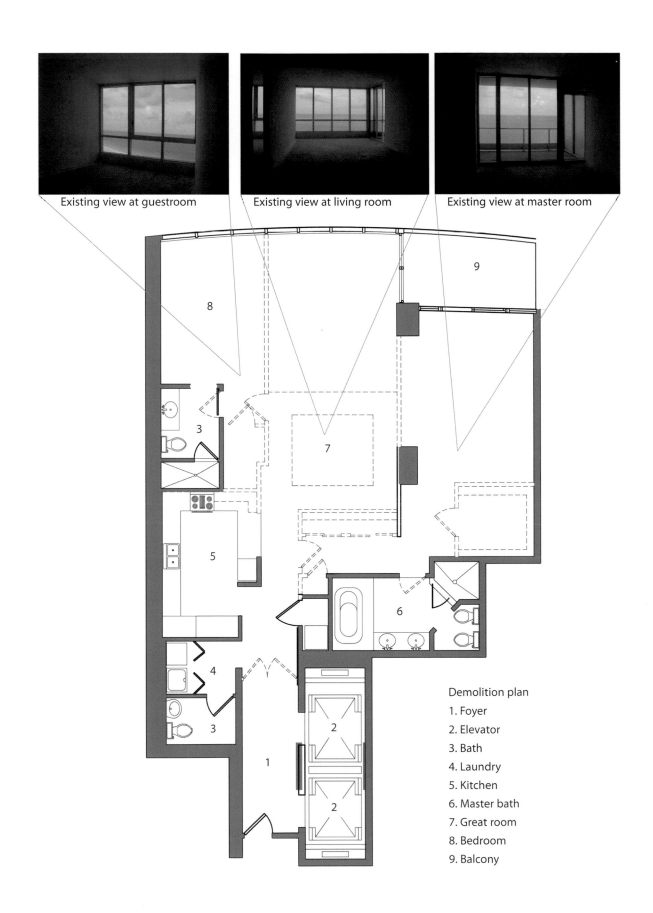

Existing view at guestroom

Existing view at living room

Existing view at master room

8

9

3

7

5

6

4

3

1

2

2

Demolition plan
1. Foyer
2. Elevator
3. Bath
4. Laundry
5. Kitchen
6. Master bath
7. Great room
8. Bedroom
9. Balcony

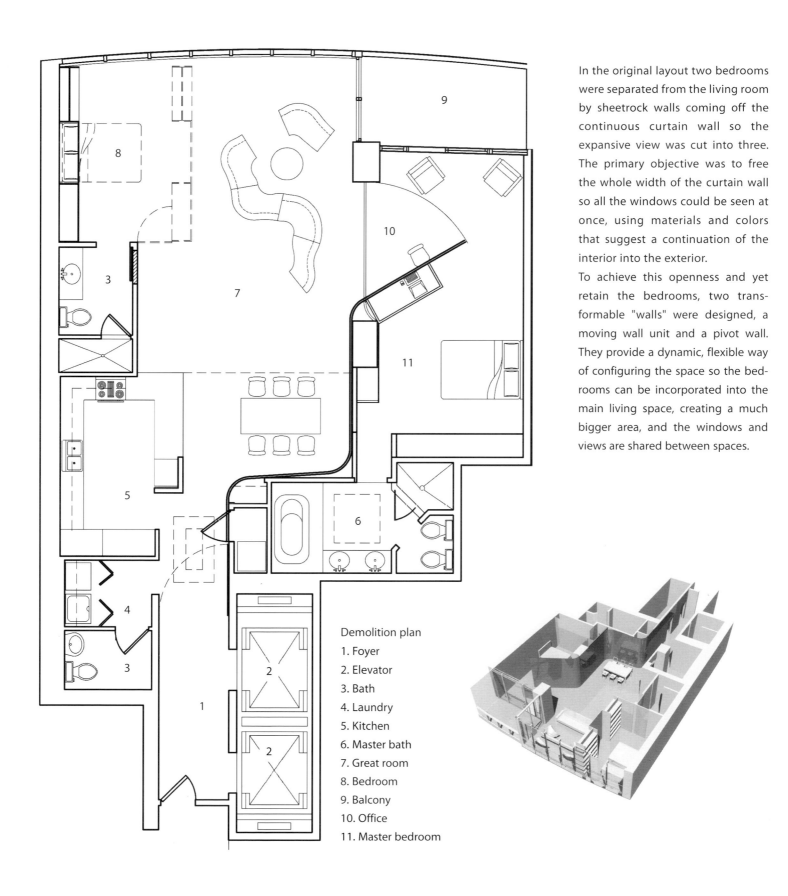

In the original layout two bedrooms were separated from the living room by sheetrock walls coming off the continuous curtain wall so the expansive view was cut into three. The primary objective was to free the whole width of the curtain wall so all the windows could be seen at once, using materials and colors that suggest a continuation of the interior into the exterior.

To achieve this openness and yet retain the bedrooms, two transformable "walls" were designed, a moving wall unit and a pivot wall. They provide a dynamic, flexible way of configuring the space so the bedrooms can be incorporated into the main living space, creating a much bigger area, and the windows and views are shared between spaces.

Demolition plan
1. Foyer
2. Elevator
3. Bath
4. Laundry
5. Kitchen
6. Master bath
7. Great room
8. Bedroom
9. Balcony
10. Office
11. Master bedroom

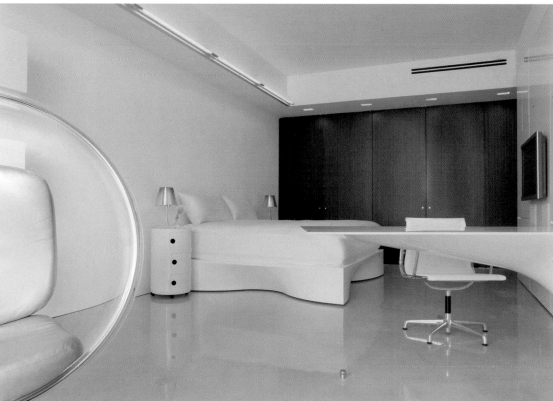

The finish materials were carefully chosen to accentuate the view and internalize the ocean, sky and sand: the blue custom Resin floor has a sand-like texture with a smooth surface while the translucent curtains enhance the blue and the glossy white walls reflect the ocean. The interior view, with its rosewood paneling and warmer colors, emphasizes solidity in contrast with the bright finishes on the ocean side.

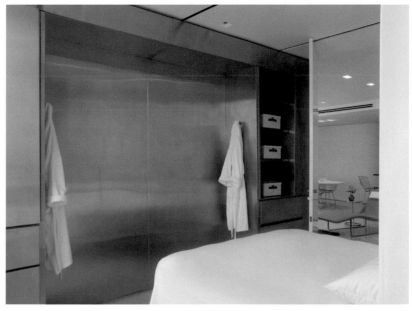

i29 office for spatial design

Heart of the home + Blossom

Dutch design company i29 are masters at maximising small spaces, creating award-winning solutions in answer to the problems of limited space. Here they outline two examples of what they describe as their leefmachines or 'living machines', their own particular brand of furniture/ interior design.

The first, known as the 'heart of the home', has transformed a compact apartment of 55sqm in Amsterdam into a luxurious home. In the centre of the apartment they designed a unit which comprises a bathroom, kitchen and storage space, all together as one object. The most important feature is that the unit is a compact box, a 'living machine', with a household around it. In this way optimal spatial experience is guaranteed. The designers' idea is that a piece of furniture like this should be custom built according to the needs of the clients, bearing in mind their way of life.

The design is minimalist and finely detailed. By integrating the different elements - the cupboards, bathroom and kitchen - it leaves the rest of the space in the apartment to be experienced as a whole. All fronts and doors have been made gripless to express the autonomy of the object. Materials and design have been carefully chosen to create a unique atmosphere. The rest of the furnishings are from Vitra, Moooi and Spectrum

This compact city apartment is divided into three zones: the front, which gives on to the street, is the kitchen, dining and socializing area; the middle area is for living and relaxing, while the back which gives on to the garden is the quiet sleeping and reading area. Although there are no walls or any dividing objects, these different areas are still very clearly defined thanks to the custom-built unit which organizes the rest of the space.

In another remarkable example of how to resolve the problem of restricted space, they have designed a unit, named Blossom, which contains a bed, toilet, shower and sink for a private home in Wassenaar in Holland. Everything about this volume is sleek and compact. Glass doors lead to the shower and toilet, both of which are finished in polyester. At the front of the unit a sink and mirror are integrated.

In a twenty-first century take on the four-poster bed a design of blossoming tree branches printed on voile surround the bed, giving the sensation of light and springtime the whole year round.

This project was presented at the VSK Baden in Holland trade fair in Utrecht. In addition i29 received an honourable mention for the interior design of this bed and bathroom at the Bathroom Design Awards 2006 in Holland which was awarded to them at the Jaarbeurs Utrecht trade fair and exhibition centre.

HEART OF THE HOME
Location:
Amsterdam, the Netherlands
Total floor area: 55 sqm
Floor:
Uni Walton, rubber coating
Walls/ceiling: plaster, white
Bathroom:
Multiplex, Polyester, Epoxy coating
Kitchen unit:
MDF, white spray painted, Bamboo multiplex
Photographs:
i29 office for spatial design

BLOSSOM
Location:
Wassenaar, the Netherlands
Total floor area: 35 sqm
Floor: wood, painted
Walls/ceiling: plaster, white
Bathroom:
Multiplex, Polyester
Bedroom:
MDF, white spray painted, printed voile
Photographs:
i29 office for spatial design

Heart of the home

Blossom

Heart of the home

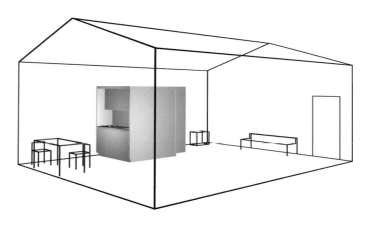

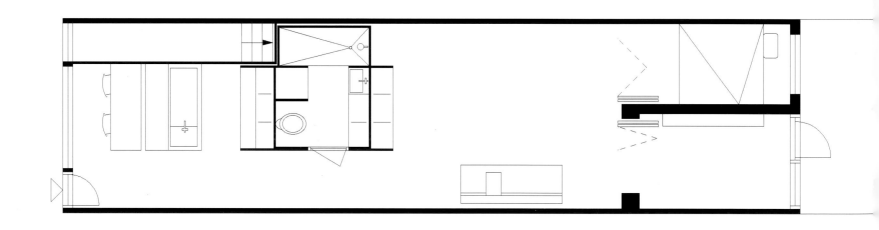

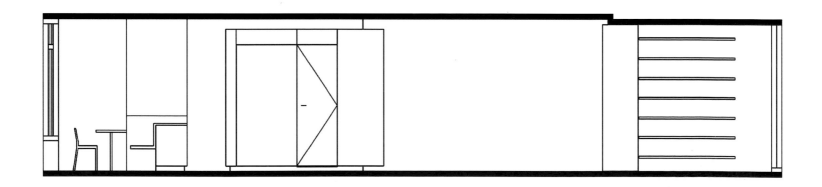

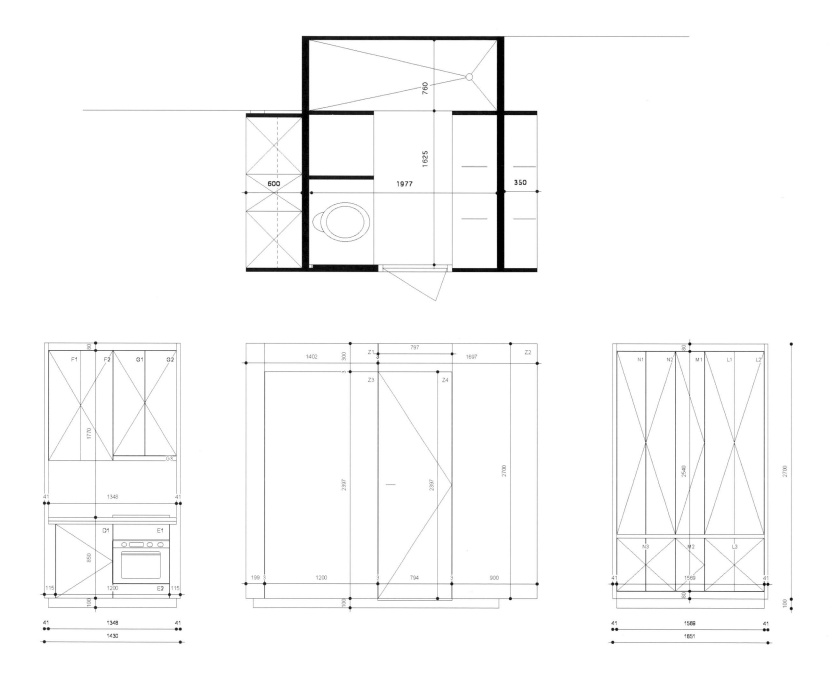

Blossom

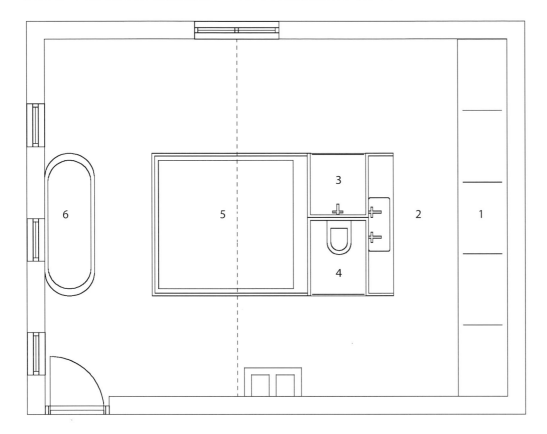

1. Wardrobe
2. Washing stand
3. Shower
4. Toliet
5. Bed
6. Bath

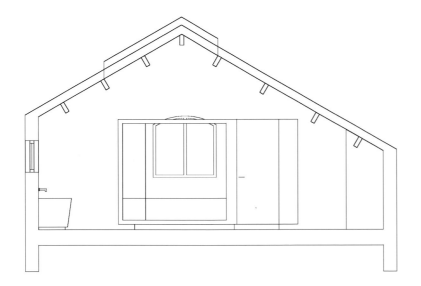

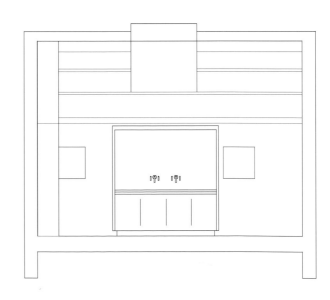

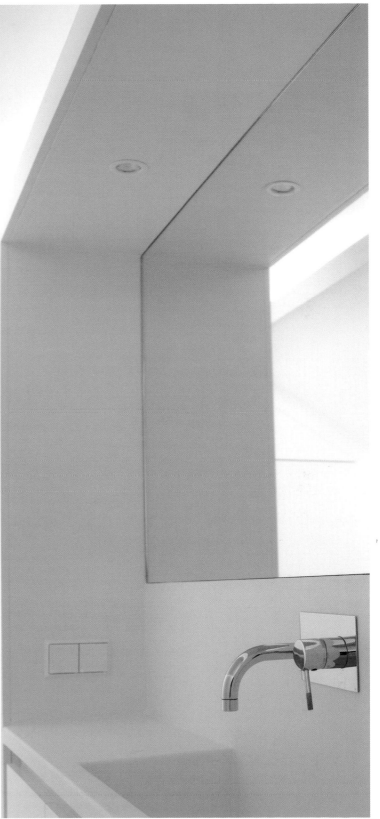

Matali Crasset

Infinite Interior - F.L.A.T.

Matali Crasset is a young French industrial designer, who spent five years working with Philippe Starck before opening her own successful studio in Paris. As we can see from this candy colored experimental apartment she has her own, extremely individual vision on living spaces. This project was selected as one of ten that formed part of the First Architectural Biennial in Beijing in 2004. Ten international designers were asked to create apartments which were later put up for sale. Crasset's fantastical contribution is situated on the seventh floor of a 31-story tower in Phoenix City, a commercial and residential complex.

According to Crasset its aim is to illustrate two ways of entering the contemporary world. This is a continual theme in her designs which try to encourage us to question the way we go about our daily lives or as she says herself "to sidestep the rigidity of our structures….question codes". She likes people to use objects and spaces in their own way.

In the case of this Beijing apartment she created a quiet space in the centre of the 2,700 square foot home which was intended to be a haven from the frenetic city outside, a connection with nature, where personal or individual activities can be pursued. It is surrounded in acid-green glass with a border of artificial trees made from birch wood. Consolidating on the natural theme the ceiling is blue to suggest the sky. It is intended to be the breathing heart of the home full of light which, like a patio, allows one to relax, get a new focus and disconnect.

The bedrooms, living and dining areas, kitchen and a second bathroom are laid out around this centre piece. Crasset's hallmark is the custom-built furniture found in these spaces, an integral part of the concept and design and an expression of her design philosophy. The desk in the central zone for example has only a few shelves built into it so that its user is able to think of other things and not be distracted by surrounding books. Functionality also plays an important part, so the electric pink master bed is associated with a work space, while the crushed raspberry colored sofa allows one to go from a relaxed position to an active one.

The child's room has a practical blue and orange melamine unit combining bed and storage in a playful design that is eminently functional. It all hangs from the wall so as to allow maximum play area on the floor. With other attractive elements like a cotton-covered foam 'nest' in a corner of the living area, a mini-greenhouse for aromatic plants in the kitchen, a mini-sauna, a meditation area and the vibrant color scheme, who wouldn't feel like a child with a new toy living in this exciting space?

Location:
Beijing, PR.China
Curator:
Alice Morgaine + Diana Chieng
Supported:
China Resources of Land Beijing Co., Ltd
Approved:
Chinese Ministry of Culture and Chinese Ministry of Construction
Photographs:
www.matalicrasset.com

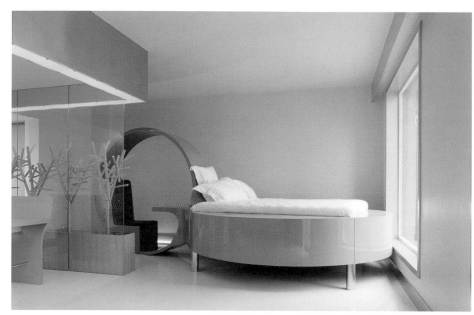

Crasset's hallmark is the custom-built furniture found in these spaces, an integral part of the concept and design and an expression of her design philosophy.

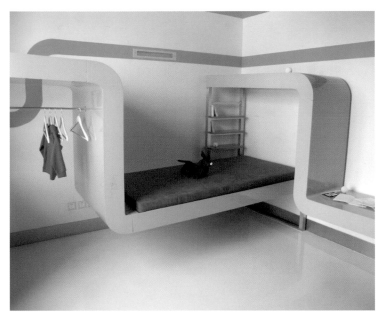

Michele Saee Studio

Infinite Interior-Template House

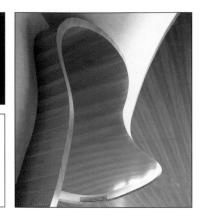

The design for the condominium in Phoenix City challenges the conventions of elemental structure and is an attempt to produce a flowing space where everyday activities take place with the least amount of resistance and clutter. The new design, conceived as a "template house", unifies the space by joining the floor, walls and ceiling into a continuous space that accommodates the functions and technical necessities of the new living organism. The space has its own flexibility and ability to be modified through shifting materials, moveable partitions, and an infinite number of templates that can be customized by each tenant. This secondary skin creates another environment that shifts and changes based on the needs and wants of the inhabitants.

The design of the house was developed in two parts: the outer container, which was the existing concrete building, and the inner container, which was the Template house. Like the body, both spaces were composed of many parts. The individual elements had to work together to ensure balance.

It all began with the idea of the template, which stemmed from the line drawings not being an accurate representation of the shapes when presented to the carpenter. Suddenly, with the line drawings, the issue became more of the nature of the lines than on what they were describing. How the line was drawn, its thickness, its errors, and so on, would become an additional determinate in the shapes rather than an actual definition. As a result of the drawing's limitations, a template was required to help move the process ahead.

The templates were made at the site from the designer's drawings by the carpenters with a simple piece of bendable wood and a pencil, then they were given to the other carpenters and the process continued, and from those templates, more templates were constructed. Once the formwork was built, sheathing began and the process continued. The sheets of plywood were bent on top of the frame to the shapes that the templates had defined and they were installed sheet by sheet. There was no template save for experimentation and eventually the success of one of the panels became the pattern for the rest.

Location:
Beijing, P.R.China
Total area:
232 sqm
Designer:
Michele Saee
Design assistant:
Franco Rosete, Zhang Haitong
Interior designer:
Michele Saee Studio
Lighting:
Michele Saee Studio
General contractor:
Sundart, Dongguan Sundart Timber Products Co.Ltd.
Photographs:
Chen SU

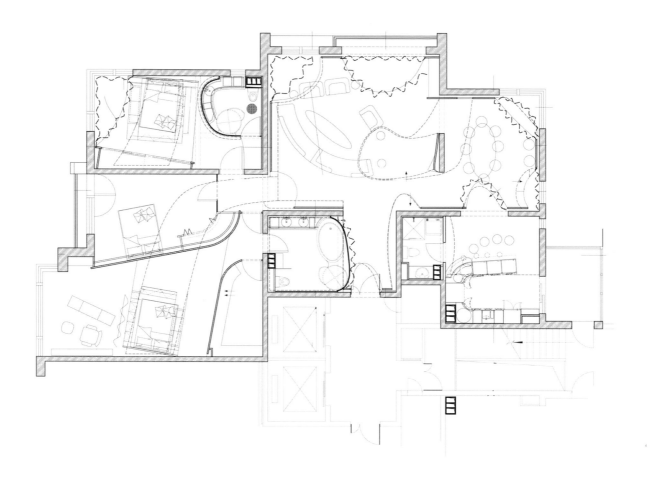

Designing and building in China was a welcoming and challenging experience for this American architect, who tried to imagine how future occupants might one day respond to this space. The design process, therefore, was eventually "surrendered to Feng Shui" as a guiding principle in achieving a sense of harmony and balance. The Ch'i, the cosmic breath, the human spirit, is that which determines our movements, our actions; Feng Shui is the rule of the Ch'i.

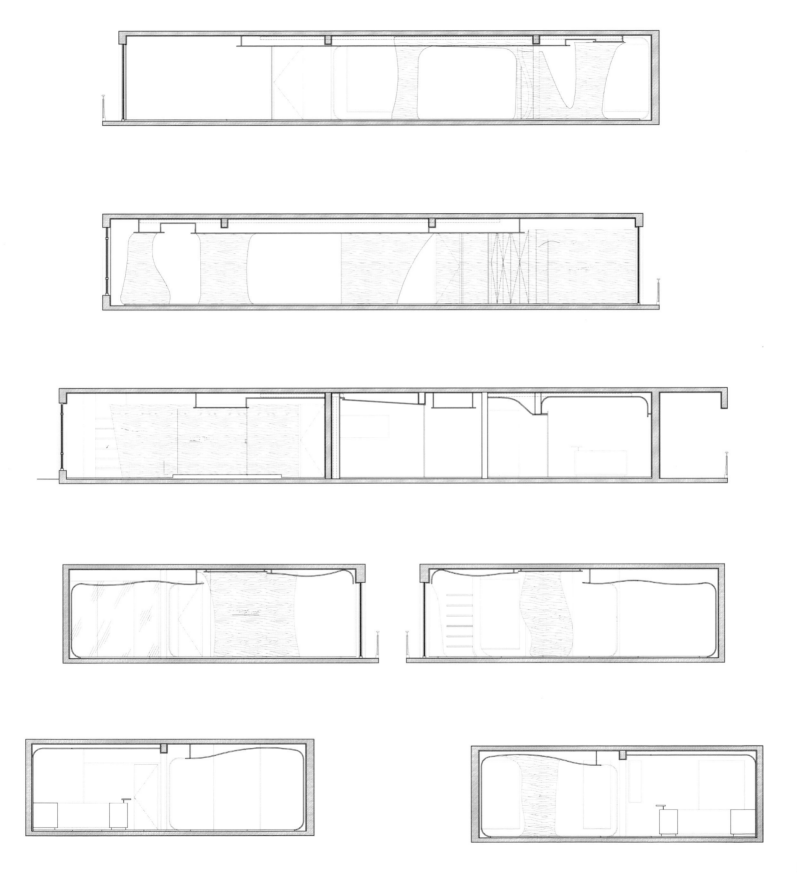

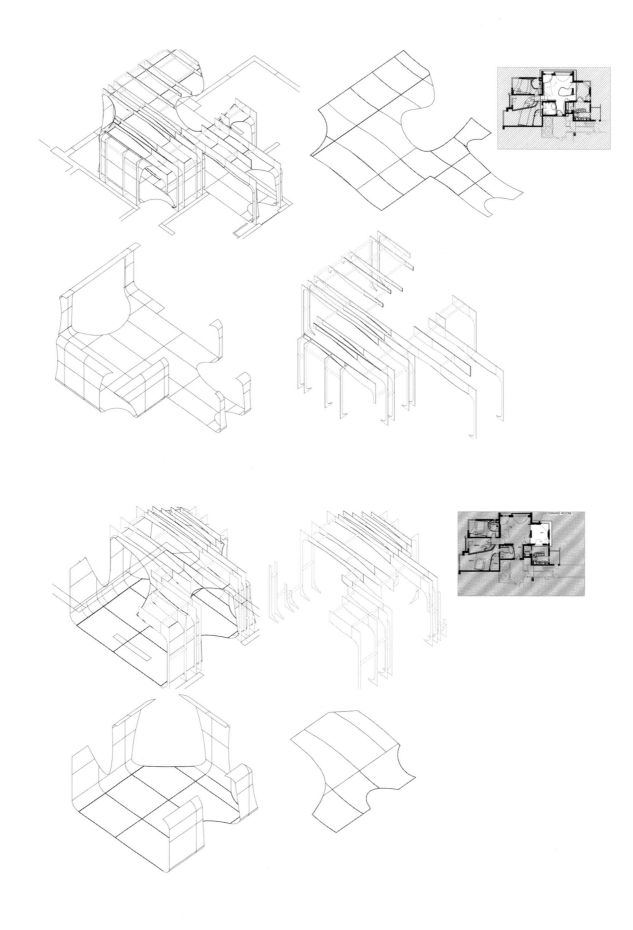

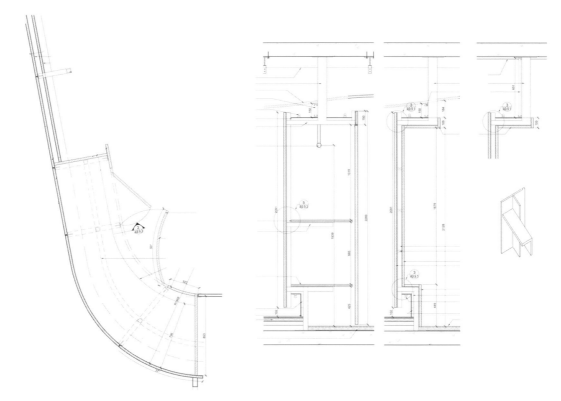

The project is one container within another; the secondary skin embodies the idea of the vessel. The design of the Template House is an experiment in whether the distinctly separate elements that work together to construct the space can be utilized in such a way that a sense of unity is achieved outside the ceiling, walls and floor combinations that normally speak of reliance upon one another, while having separate roles in the space.

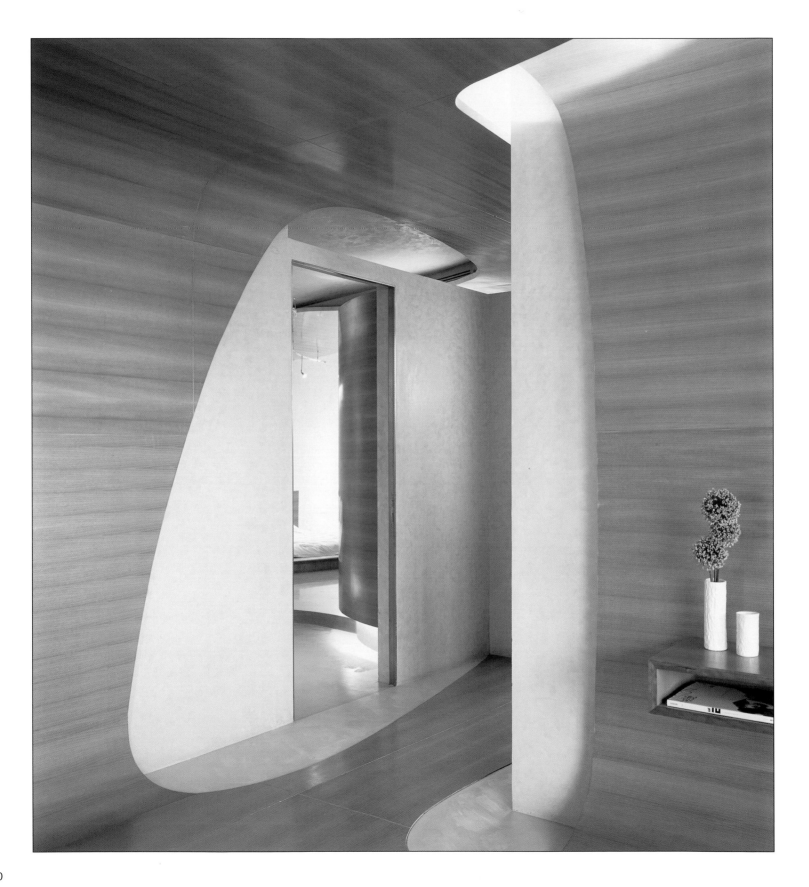

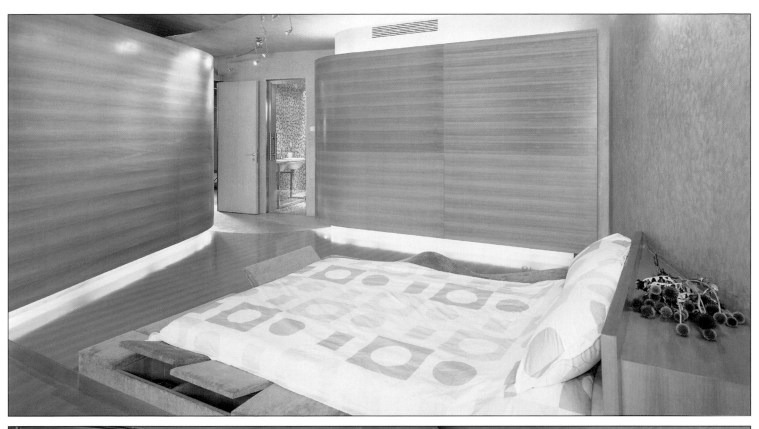

Hanrahan Meyers architects

White Space

'White Space' is a 1600 square foot apartment in Manhattan, on Central Park West. The objective was to renovate a two bedroom, two-bath apartment that was sliced into several small rooms by opening the space to light and air, and to create a focus toward the views of Central Park.

The existing space was gutted and the second bath altered to become the master bath, with a translucent glass wall facing the living room, allowing the sense of the windows and views to the Park through the glass.

The ceiling was a major aspect of the design. Originally a random grid of irregularly placed structural beams, it was re-designed as a free-form composition to work in harmony with the new opened up floor plan. Most of it was dropped to the height of the bottom of the beams, but with holes cut into it incorporating light fixtures. As an overall design it has become part of an abstract, painterly composition pulling the lines of the new apartment together into a new gestalt.

Wood panels placed on the uneven south wall create storage and, at the same time, straighten the wall. At the western edge of this wall, the surface becomes lower, and turns into an area of low storage units with stainless steel shelves above. A free-form piece of ash sits on these low cabinets, making a counter.

The existing kitchen is on a raised area near the entrance, separated by a wall which the architects removed to create a new modernist kitchen with cabinets to match the wood panels in the rest of the apartment. A freestanding translucent glass wall separates the kitchen from the dining area and entrance space.

The dining table is a continuation of the kitchen counter, becoming ash as it passes through the glass wall. As this area was too small to allow seating on both sides of the table the Architects installed a clear structural glass floor extension which allows dining table seating to extend into the living room. The glass floor floats above a free-form ash step, connecting the entrance to the living area.

The bedroom is lined with painted wood panels and plaster surfaces. Architect-designed bedroom furniture is made from wire brushed solid wood with a high gloss white lacquer finish. A free-form piece of ash sits on top of the bed headboard.

Originating from a conversation about Kasmir Malevich's painting, 'White on White' the apartment was designed as a white box, based on a series of whites but kept rich by varying the texture and the materiality of the white elements. The variations are created by sandblasted, painted wood; wire brushed painted wood; matte and polished plaster walls; floors whitened by bleaching and staining over oak plank; and floors finished with honed white marble tile. Floating within the white box, large pieces of free-form ash reference nature.

The end result is a space that flows and accommodates the needs for living with a great sense of comfort and warmth while the focus is on Central Park.

Location:
New York, USA
Design Team:
Victoria Meyers, Thomas Hanrahan, Kathy Chang, Dan Cheong
Lighting Designer:
Richard Shaver
General Contractor:
Fountainhead Construction, Steve Abrahms
Square Footage:
1600 square feet
Photographs:
Michael Moran

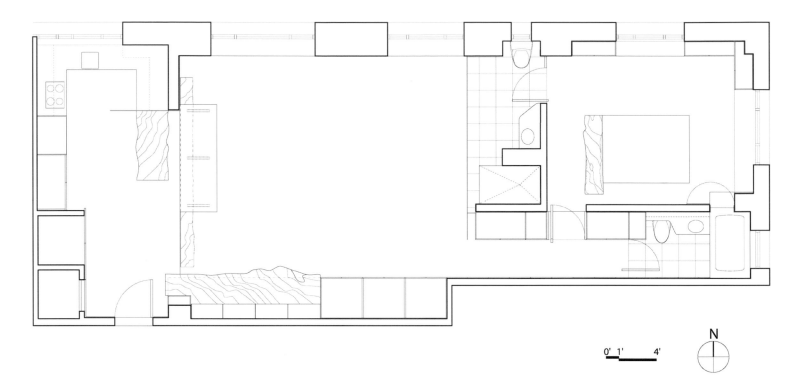

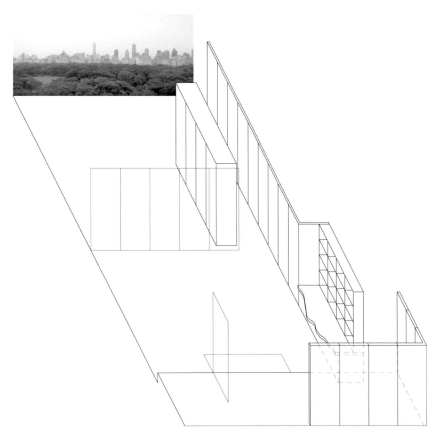

The dining table is a continuation of the kitchen counter, becoming ash as it passes through the glass wall. As this area was too small to allow seating on both sides of the table the Architects installed a clear structural glass floor extension which allows dining table seating to extend into the living room. The glass floor floats above a free-form ash step, connecting the entrance to the living area.

Francesco Rota

Apartment in Milan

Belonging to a renowned collector of contemporary art, this apartment is located in a small town on the outskirts of Milan. It has a modern, representative ambience in which the client enjoys all the desired comforts and has space for entertaining numerous guests.

The floor plan occupies two levels and has a total of approximately 400 square meters. The entryway on the lower floor leads to the completely diaphanous daytime zone, where the only partitions are those that enclose the closet – and these have been lightened by vertical incisions that provide glimpses of the interior. The living room is well lit by a large oblong window.

The large corner sofa, designed by the architect Francesco Rota, is composed of various separate modules that can be grouped in different arrangements to suit the needs of any given moment. The audio/visual installation is set into a hanging shelf unit done partly in rosewood.

One part of the living room is intended as a lounge area. Two armchairs that can be joined to create a single surface are set in front of the fireplace, which was designed by the architects themselves.

A long anodized aluminum table and cupboards and sand-colored chairs were chosen for the dining room.

The kitchen, which is open to the dining room, is a spacious and functional room. The color of the furniture contrasts with the white of the walls and the dark tone of the wood flooring. The floor-to-ceiling door is of transparent glass. The opening set into the wall with the stairwell leads to the guest room, which has its own bathroom.

A long flight of stairs in steel and glass leads to the upper floor and is lit from above by multi-colored fluorescent tubes that create an interplay of lighting effects via Zumtobel's Luxmate system. A remote control allows the client to choose the tones that will light this area, as well as activate a system of dynamic lighting. The installation is concealed behind a translucent suspended ceiling that enhances the variations of light and color.

Upstairs, two sliding doors consisting of two sheets of transparent glass, each in a different color, provide entry to, respectively, the study, which leads to the bedroom, and a workout room, which is connected to the laundry room. Sliding doors were chosen so as to enable the creation of a single space when they are left open.

With its shower accessed on one side from the bedroom or, on the other, the workout room, the bathroom is the centerpiece on this floor. It is entirely clad in back-painted glass, black in the shower and sink, and white for the bath, which has a hydro-massage feature.

Location:
Milan, Italy
Photographs:
Stefania Giorgi

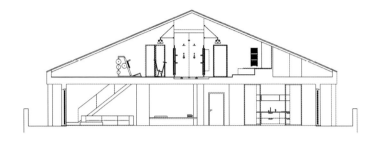

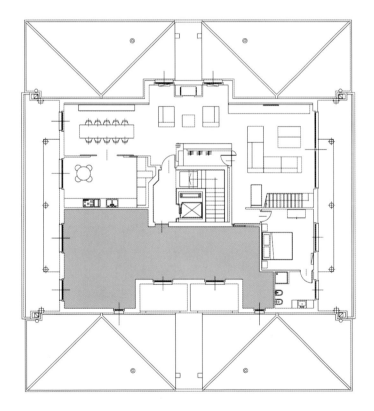

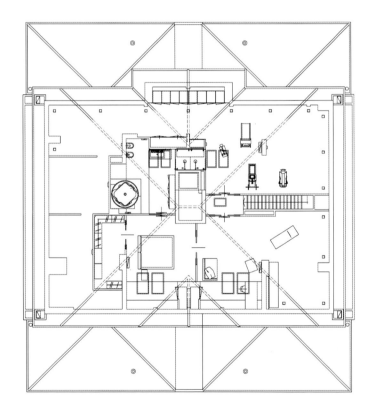

Lower floor plan

Upper floor plan

Rosewood was chosen for all of the furniture designed for this home; its dark hue forms a counterpoint to the orange of the bed, the red of the armchairs and especially to the white of most of the walls.

All of the lamps are designers' pieces; some were created by the architect himself.

Unique one-off objects acquired on various trips as well as contemporary artwork provide the personalized touch in this refined setting.

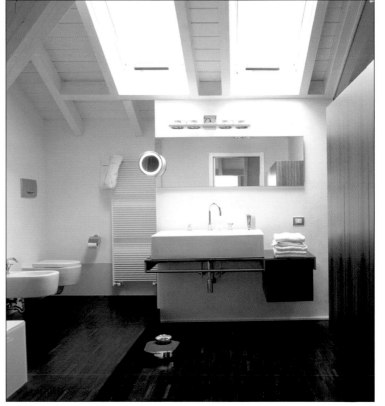

Agustí Costa

Duplex in Berga

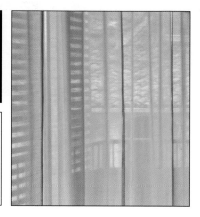

This duplex flat is in the small town of Berga, in the Pyrenean foothills. It occupies part of the 3rd and 4th floor of a new residential building. The drainage installation determined where the bathrooms and the kitchen would go, together with much of the the lower floor. Viable decisions were directed to articulating mobility and improving the penetration of natural light. The client required privacy for the three bedrooms, and a private bathroom for the master bedroom. The rest of the space could have an open plan distribution, i.e., the hall, the diningroom-livingroom, the kitchen, a bathroom on the lower floor, and an attic studio with a terrace.

Location:
Berga, Spain
Photographs:
David Cardelús

A complete glass wall, backlit at night, replaced the little window onto the lightwell, and a large zenithal skylight was introduced, with views towards the mountains.

In the entrance hall, the color of the walls goes from white to gray to black, announcing the ranges that obtain in the rest of the flat. The floors are of solid oak. The stairs to the studio reflect the character of wooden attic stairs in the vernacular local houses; raised one centimeter off the floor, it reaches the upper floor without resting on it, leaving a slender gap to state the stair's autonomy regarding the building.

Frameless sheets of glass move on runners to close the kitchen and dining room doors. The kitchen side is frosted, the other is transparent, to allow visibility through the hall, the living room and the terrace, and out into the street. The double height of the dining and living-room area is topped by a sloped ceiling in response to the roof above. On the kitchen side, the double height doesn't exist, so the baluster has been omitted to allow visual access to the studio. This space, with the richness of undefined things, is open to a variety of functions.

The project relies on the homogenous treatment and equivalent value of the different items. Identical materials for the built-in furniture and the same color on all the walls and ceilings, contribute to the overall effect of serenity. The curtains and some structural members are brightly colored, casting indirect light of various hues that change throughout the day. Warm toned fluorescent lights recessed in the ceiling, floodlit walls and flexible standing lamps (Tolomeo) resolve the subtle lighting installation.

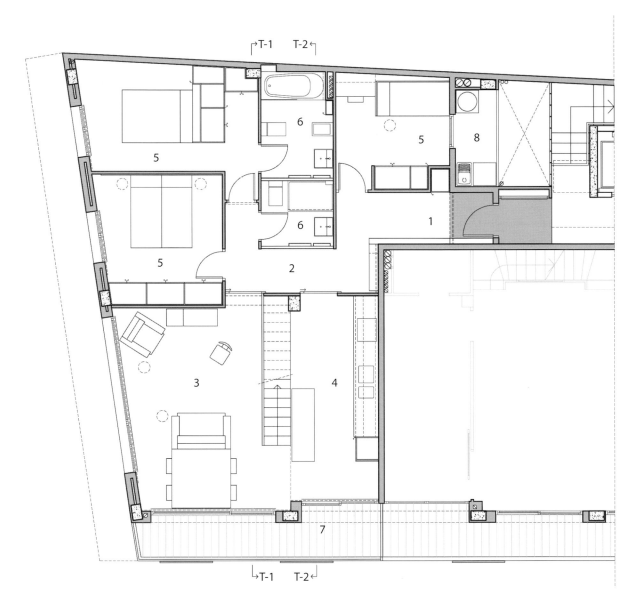

Living floor plan

1. Entry
2. Corridor
3. Living-dining room
4. Kitchen
5. Bedroom
6. Bathroom
7. Balcony
8. Laundry

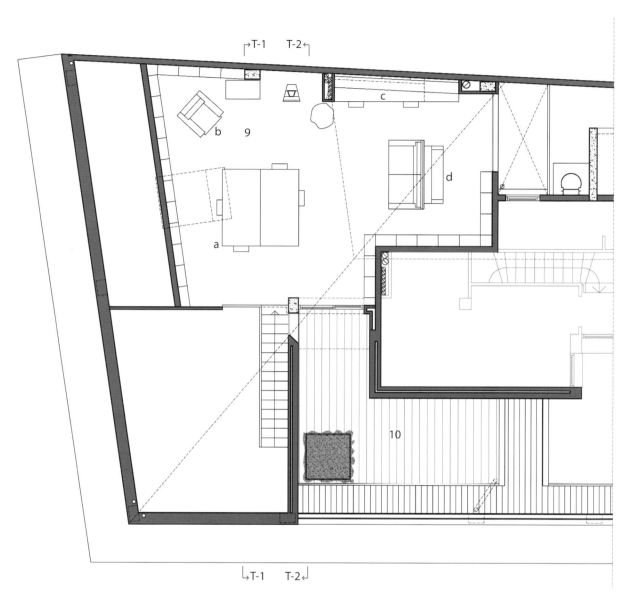

T-1   T-2

T-1   T-2

Duplex floor plan
 9. Studio
        a. Mobile table
        b. Reading
        c. Fixed table
        d. Piano
10. Terrace

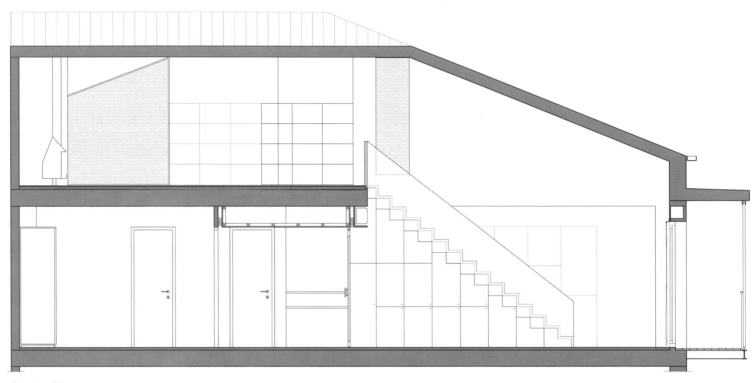

Section T-1

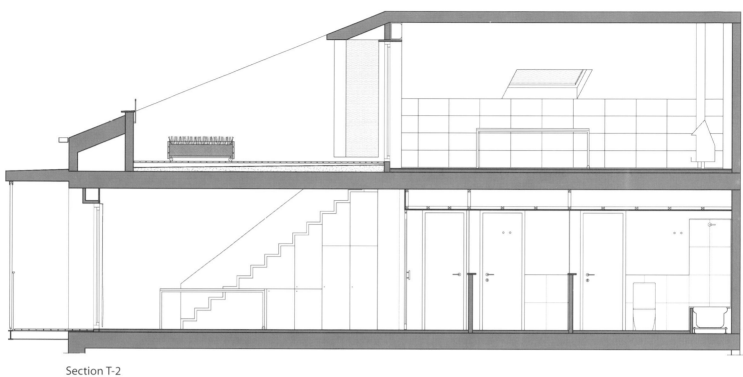

Section T-2

The stairs to the studio reflect the character of wooden attic stairs in the vernacular local houses; raised one centimeter off the floor, it reaches the upper floor without resting on it, leaving a slender gap to state the stair's autonomy regarding the building.

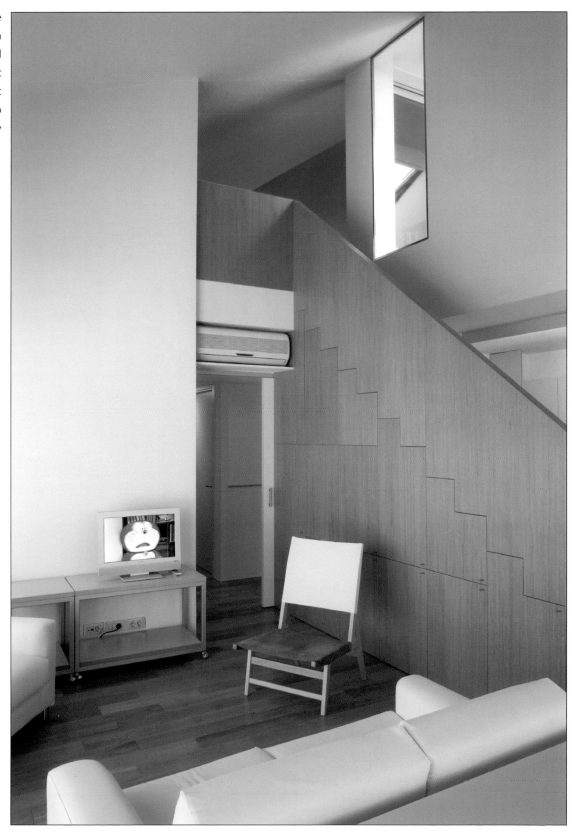

Tommie Wilhelmsen

Villa Joaalle

Completed in January 2006, Villa Joaalle is a 2260 sqft (210 sqmt) family house, on two floors. The house is located on a typical site at the edge of a suburban area consisting mainly of villas built in the 1980s. The site is open to an extensive landscape of green fields that stretch away to the west.

The upper level of the house is one big room of 110sqm. The living room, dining room, kitchen and entrance are all in the one same space. The lower level contains the bedrooms, the bathroom, a workroom and storage space. The house is built of wood and reinforced concrete, with aluminum-framed windows to the exterior.

The outdoor terrace and living room are on the same level, and are perceived as one big uninterrupted floor space. The house presents a closed façade against north, but is open to the south and west to take in as much daylight as possible, as well as to include the landscape in the interior of the living room.

The formal decisions and the materials chosen are clear and raw, with simple, straightforward joints and finishes. Structurally, one big folding sheet of concrete, insulation layers, ductwork and other systems defines the character of the house, both inside and outside. Only a difference in the finish of the surface of the alcove in the sitting room indicates an intermediate space between in and out. The color scheme ranges abruptly between various shades of white and various shades of dark brown, such as the kitchen cabinetwork or the rust-colored steel coffee tables in the sitting room. The whole house has lighting fixtures embedded in the ceilings, and large standing lamps provide the extra light needed to illuminate a specific task. A horizontal niche let into the wall between the sitting room and the space behind houses a small fireplace and enough stored firewood to feed the fire for the evening. One of the few openings on the northern façade allows light into the stairway, which has not been encumbered with a railing to avoid spoiling its outline. The steps and the risers are all of the same material, continuing the flooring finish of the main room upstairs, and introducing a similar character into the more intimate rooms downstairs.

Location:
Norway
Surface:
2260 sqft (210 sqm)
End of construction:
January 2006
Photographs:
Tommie Wilhelmsen

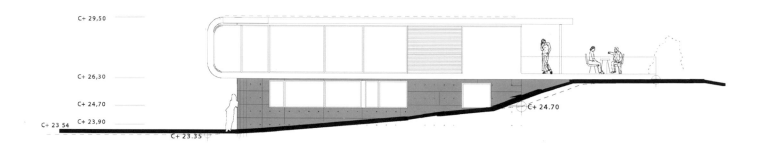

C+ 29,50

C+ 26,30

C+ 24,70

C+ 23 54   C+ 23,90

C+ 23.35

C+ 24.70

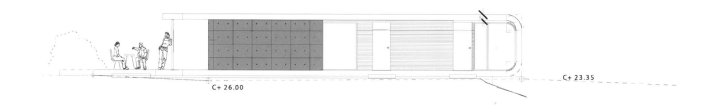

C+ 26.00

C+ 23.35

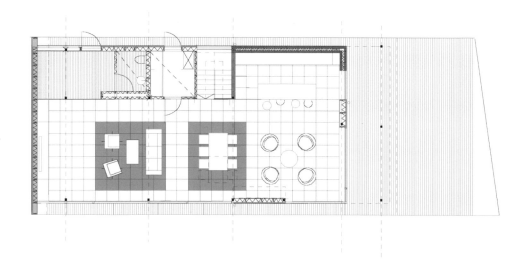

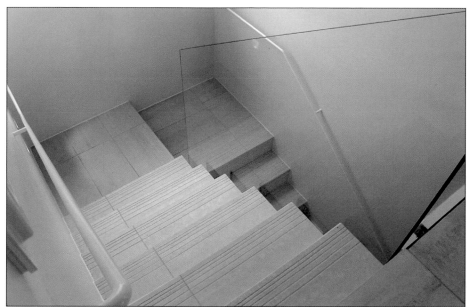

The Apartment

The Apartment YMCA

Superlatively revamped and reconstructed, what was once a YMCA basketball court and suspended running truck has been transformed into a sprawling 650 sqm design loft. Exquisitely outfitted with furniture from the world's most exclusive design studios, what had previously been presented as a raw construction zone is now an architectural and cultural showcase.

The existing trusses throughout the space hint at the former use of this elegant loft, while the rehauled interior features expanded window openings for a fresher, lighter ambience. The hardwood floor of the old basketball court was also reused, now gracing the private areas of the apartment. Poured concrete is the minimalist flooring chosen for the shared spaces.

Comfort and style were central concerns, as evidenced by the computer controlled lighting, heating and air conditioning systems and sound-insulated floor slabs. No detail was left unattended to in the kitchen, with its Corian countertops and integrated garbage disposal, wine refrigerator, two full-sized refrigerators and two dishwashers.

The apartment enjoys a total of five bedrooms and, in another measure ensuring the maximum degree of comfort, five corresponding full bathrooms. Furthermore, there are two home theaters, a home office and an indoor garden equipped with grow lights.

The master bedroom has three built-in closets and a king-sized walnut bed on a built-in platform. The six-sided, fully tiled master bathroom features two Boffi showers designed by Marcel Wanders, a steam room for two, a freestanding bathtub by Phillipe Starck, and a wall-sized medicine cabinet. A revolving disco ball adds a touch of whimsy in the sprawling walk-in master closet, where the shoe racks can accommodate 100 pairs and where there is a also a built-in vanity and a daybed.

A plush five-person sofa sits opposite a gas fireplace in the great room, which is equipped with floor outlets, an iPod docking station, DJ input station, home theater, concealed kitchenette and a moss rug by Kasthall.

Location:
New York, USA
Photographs:
Contributed by The Apartment
www.theapt.com

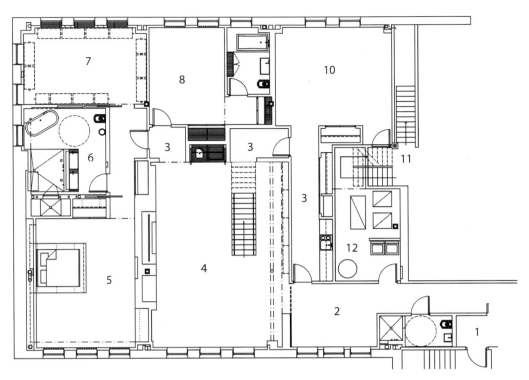

First floor plan

1. Lobby
2. Entry
3. Hall
4. Living room
5. Master bedroom
6. Master bathroom
7. Master closet
8. Bedroom
9. Bathroom
10. Design room
11. Fire stair
12. Mechanical room

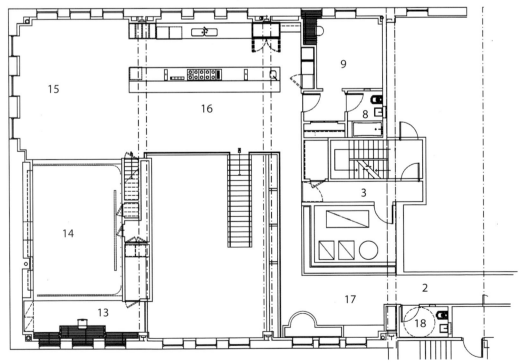

Second floor plan

13. Office
14. Home theater
15. Formal dining
16. Kitchen
17. Garden
18. Powder

Third floor plan

19. Mezzanine bedroom
20. Mezzanine bathroom
21. Open to below

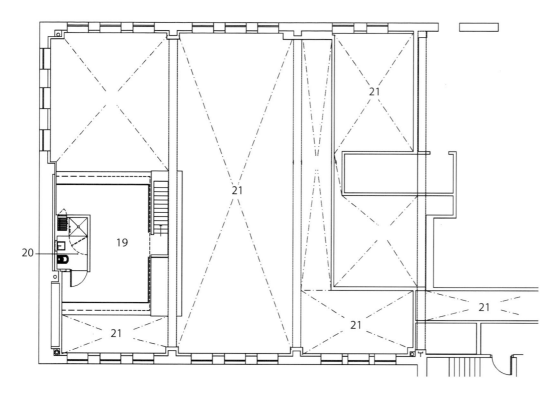

carlorattiassociati

Cinato Penthouse

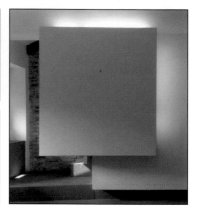

The refurbishment of a penthouse in Turin, Italy, was the opportunity to test innovative Computer Aided Design/Computer Aided Manufacturing (CAD/CAM) procedures. Digital-minimal: This project sets out to demonstrate how to take advantage of new creative techniques in architecture without producing blobs or funny shapes. Several hundred pieces, each one different from the other, were designed to fit into the existing space. The items where then manufactured out of folded and laser-cut corten steel plate. Finally and magically, all the parts were assembled into a coherent whole within the old walls.

The project was prompted by a new Italian law, which allows owners to convert spaces under the roof into penthouses. A young and liberal Turin couple, both of whom are employed in the high-tech sector, owned the top floor of a multi-story condominium in the city center. They decided to substantially increase the available footage of their property, if necessary by unconventional means. Their initial brief for the reform operation included two new bathrooms and a new staircase to access the roof. The challenging design puzzle that arose was the following: would it be possible to combine all of them into a single architectural element? The bathroom might become a staircase. But could a staircase become a bathroom?

At the entrance level, a large living room opened up, to host the owner's social activities. With a uniform corten steel floor, protected by an epoxy layer, a flexible living room for partying was created. On the upper level, industrial wood flooring was provided, to produce a more private, but equally multifunctional space.

On those occasions in which the new shape met with the original building's structural elements, these were allowed to speak for themselves, expressing a fertile dialogue between the old handcrafted materials and the digital logic of the new forms. The existing structure's functional validity was multiplied by sidestepping the routine of established types of distribution.

Location:
Turin, Italy
Design:
carlorattiassociati
Chiara Morandini, Walter Nicolino,
Carlo Ratti
Architectural design team:
Walter Nicolino, Chiara Morandini,
Anna Frisa, Carlo Ratti
Structural design:
Studio Vittorio Neirotti, Turin, Italy
Construction:
Impresa Carriere
End of construction:
2005
Photographs:
Pino dell'Aquila

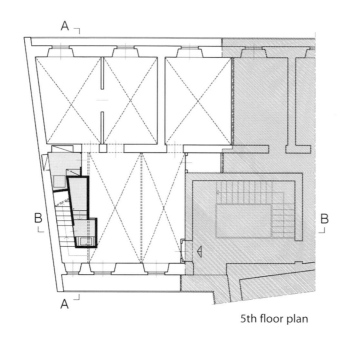

5th floor plan

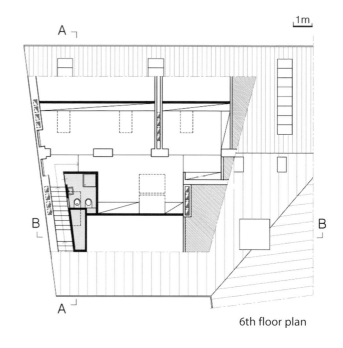

6th floor plan

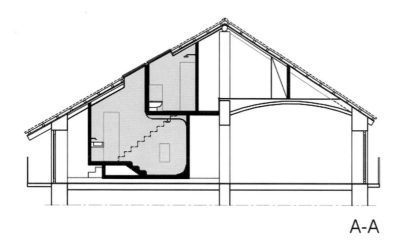

A-A

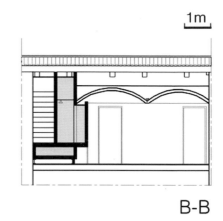

1m

B-B

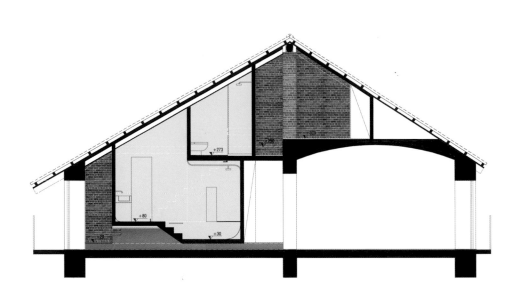

Attilio Stocchi

Loft in Ciserano

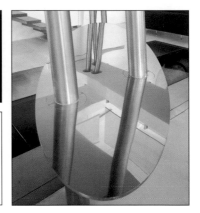

A former industrial nave near Bergamo has been converted into a roomy, modern loft. Only two of the six bays have been used in the creation of a space measuring 120 square meters, with an additional 40 square meters of intermediate floors.

The living room, dining room and kitchen are all on the ground floor, with the bathrooms and wardrobe distributed along the sides. Here, there is also space for a shower, which is located at one of the ground floor's corners and opens directly into the main room, although shielded by the steps of the straight staircase.

Downstairs, in the place originally intended for a swimming pool (the client decided to forego finishing the pool for fear of the deleterious effects of damp), is a metal sculpture measuring over ten meters in length. More than adornment, the poles that pierce the horizontal planes in an asymmetrical and concentrated way support the system of the intermediate floors. In their trajectory through the floors, some of them hold elements in place, while others simply accentuate the feeling of vertical amplitude.

The intermediate floor, with its reinforced concrete slabs, has been split into two parts: the bedroom and wardrobe, accessed by a helix-shaped stairwell. The spaces are linked by a white, slightly inclined bridge formed by a single metal plate.

With a marble bath and glass door, the bathroom is a perfect place for lying down and contemplating the front space.

Location:
Ciserano, Bergamo, Italy
Project manager:
Attilio Stocchi
studio di architettura attilio stocchi
Collaborators:
Laura Molendini, Grazia Poli
Structural design:
Evelino Facchinetti
Project:
1999
End of construction:
March 2002
Total cost:
200.000 €
Surface:
160 sqm
Photographs:
Andrea Martiradonna
studio Attilio Stocchi

©Andrea Martiradonna

117

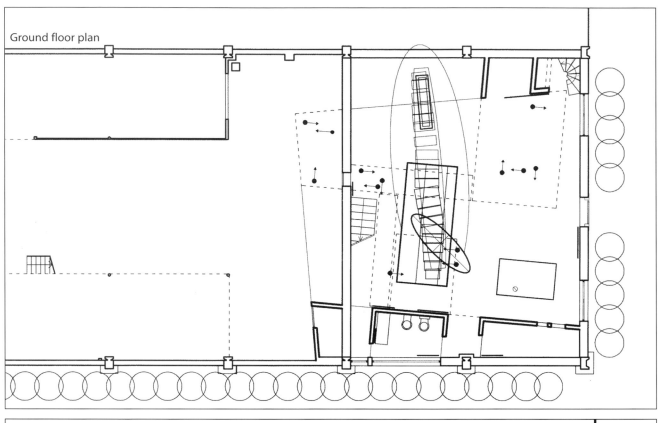

Ground floor plan

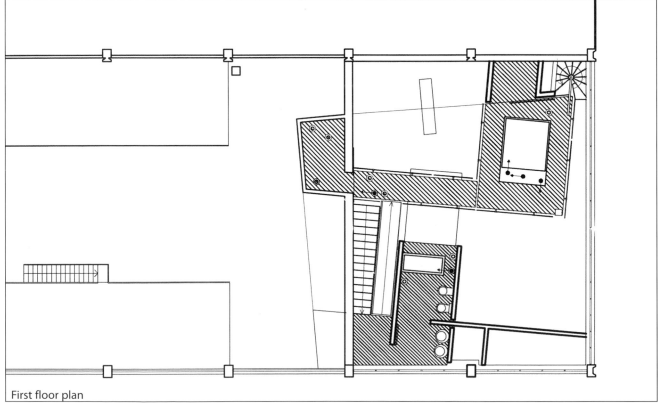

First floor plan

© studio Attilio Stocchi

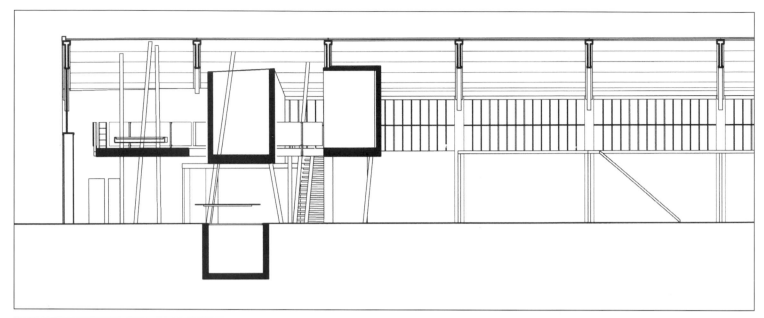

© studio Attilio Stocchi

© studio Attilio Stocchi

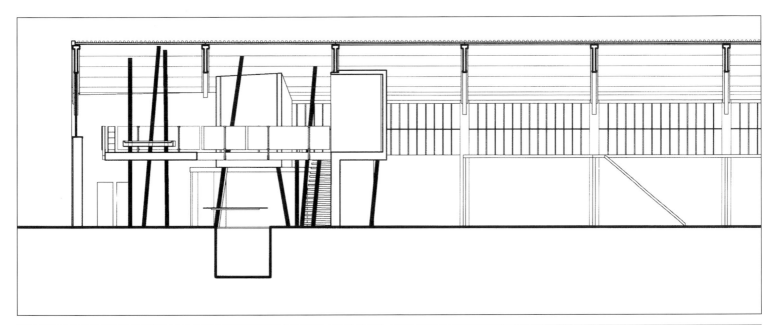

© studio Attilio Stocchi

© studio Attilio Stocchi

©Andrea Martiradonna

©Andrea Martiradonna

©Andrea Martiradonna

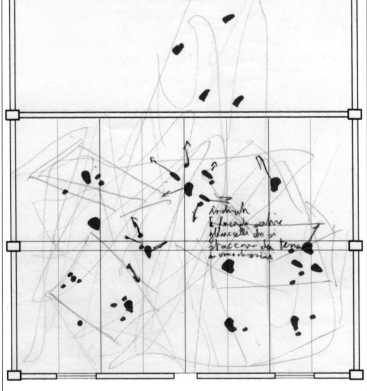

©Andrea Martiradonna

124

© studio Attilio Stocchi

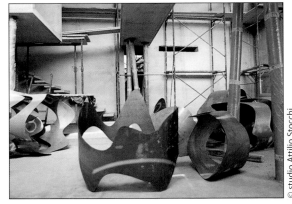
© studio Attilio Stocchi

©Andrea Martiradonna

©Andrea Martiradonna

© studio Attilio Stocchi

Nathalie Wolberg

House Atelier in Saint-Ouen

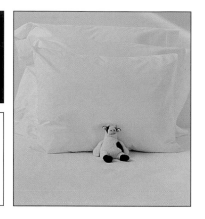

A factory from the fifties has been transformed into nine artists' studios. One of them occupies 180 sqm (+ 80 sqm of terrace) on three levels. It is the live-and-work space of the architect Nathalie Wolberg, who adjusts her designs to the client's personality, her own in this case.

Occasionally she would want the main stage emptied of all functions, becoming the void space of creation, where anything is possible. This led to the concept of the "Furniture Rooms" in response to the need for variable functions, permitting space to be managed in different scales, global, zonal or elemental). Each scale has a different social dimension, a free space, a social space, a personal space.

The "Furniture Rooms" consists of a fixed part, along the walls, which integrates the functions (light, sound,....), and a mobile part. Each space is a gadget demanding to be used. The furniture is in fact the structure of the project, the walls of the house. Variable widths, angles and colors break the monotony. The project is aimed at physical and psychological comfort, an architecture that will help people to loosen their constraining habits and rediscover a new meaning to everyday life.

From the entrance, a stairway leads up to the studio and the terrace on the first floor. The concave steps are an invitation to sit and meditate, enjoying the view.

Straight ahead, the main stage spreads out. Within it are places to share, like the dining table near the kitchen, or intimate corners like the library or the bathrooms. The bedroom is wide open but can close up like a cocoon. At the end, stairs lead down into a double height space (separated from above by a tempting safety net). At present it is used for occasional art exhibitions.

The apartment reacts to changing weather conditions. When the sun shines, the yellow walls bounce the light to the bottom of the exhibition space (space R-1); when it rains, raindrops on the windows are reflected upon the textile screens; when it is grey, the artificial lighting creates an immaterial sense of space; at night, the pink light of the screens envelops everything.

The luminous screens of translucent cloth are mobile. Drawn up, they make stripes of light, drawn down they close off an area, allowing for functional redistributions and a different reading of the global area.

Location:
Saint-Ouen, France
Architect:
Nathalie Wolberg
End of construction:
2004
Total floor area:
180 sqm (+ 80 sqm terrace)
Photographs:
Gaelle Le Boulicaut

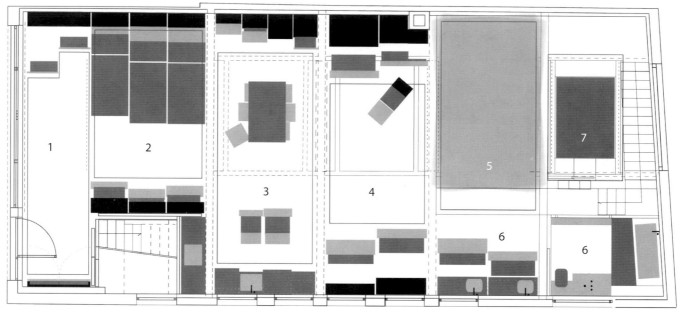

Ground floor plan

1. Entrance
2. Living room
3. Kitchen - Dining room
4. Reading
5. Relax room
6. Bathroom
7. Bedroom

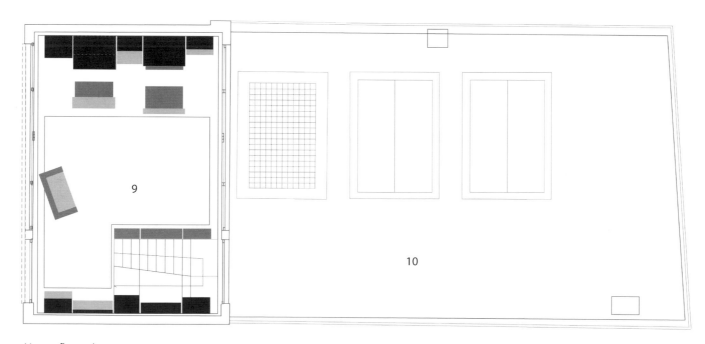

Upper floor plan

9. Study
10. Terrace

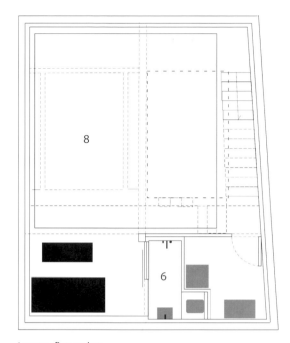

Lower floor plan
6. Bathroom
8. Exhibition room

Cross section: Study

Cross section: Entrance

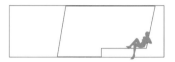

Cross section: Living room

Cross section: Kitchen - Dining room

Cross section: Reading

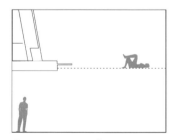

Cross section: Relax room
Exhibition room

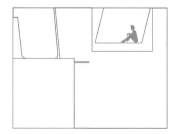

Cross section: Bedroom
Exhibition room

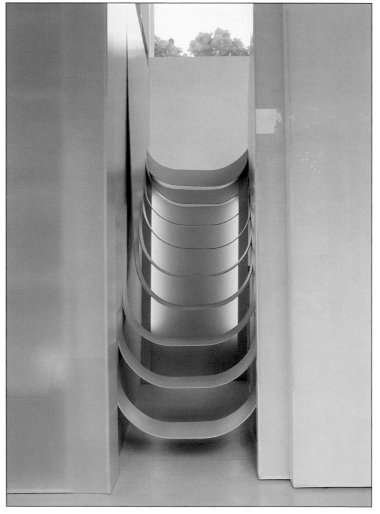

Johannes Will

City Lounge

The renovation of this 150-square-meter apartment in an old building required the initial removal of numerous walls and openings in order to bring the general layout into line with modern standards of spaciousness.

The key word governing the design from that point on was "reduction" – the breaking down of elements and living spaces into their essential functions to allow nothing more than the interplay of light and shadows to determine the character of each space. Paradoxically, this restraint in design is precisely that which lends particular weight and effectiveness to each element, which is allowed to speak for itself.

See, for example, the almost jarring fragmentation of the main wall, one of whose openings is glazed, to create passageways without the need for doors between the bathroom-kitchen zone and living room. The sculptural form of this wall naturally gave rise to the creation here of shelving, which also lends structure to this large space. A further example of the desire to reduce elements to their essentials is seen in the importance of changing lighting conditions in the home throughout the day and how they interact with the meticulously-chosen and simplified materials: glass, aluminum, nut parquet flooring and sliding oak panels.

All of the kitchen appliances, washing machine and dishwasher can be concealed by sliding panels when not in use, creating an impression of continuity that is further enhanced by the absence of joints, doors and, by extension, door handles.

Resin panels ordinarily employed in shipbuilding were used in place of tiling in the bathroom, which is the culminating point of a communication zone originating at the kitchen block. This zone not only joins the spaces, but also provides the setting where guests might interact.

The bedrooms, on the other hand, have been designed to avoid such chance encounters and are screened off from the main living area. A floor-to-ceiling sliding element pushes away to reveal the hall that distributes the bedrooms. A dramatic opaque curtain-like element shields the main bedroom from light and views in from the outside.

Location:
Vienna, Austria

Size:
150 sqm

Start of planning:
January 2004

Start of construction:
April 2004

Completion of project:
August 2004

Photographs:
Paul Ott

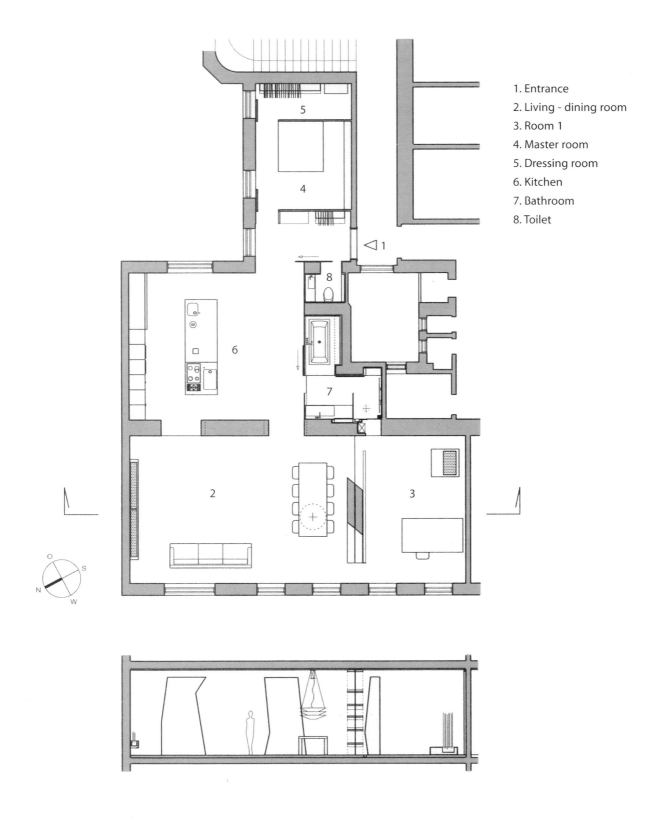

1. Entrance
2. Living - dining room
3. Room 1
4. Master room
5. Dressing room
6. Kitchen
7. Bathroom
8. Toilet

All of the kitchen appliances, washing machine and dishwasher can be concealed by sliding panels when not in use, creating an impression of continuity that is further enhanced by the absence of joints, doors and, by extension, door handles.

Michele Bonino, Subhash Mukerjee

Apartment in Torino

A small, but unusually deep two-floor house is overshadowed among the massive buildings that have arisen all around it, in the Primo Governo period.

The building contains a 100 sqm apartment that needs to make the most of a limited amount of natural light available.

Accepting the lack of light within the central core of the building, this is kept dark on purpose, while its outer "shell" is designed to reflect the natural light powerfully throughout all the inner spaces.

The staircase that descends from the roof functions as a giant skylight. One of the showers is held by a structure suspended from the roof; direct natural light floods in through a skylight; the shower is provided with a translucent glass floor, which throws an agreeable light over the work desk below.

When the need is felt for a more direct contact with the environment, a 60 sqm roof terrace is a convenient extra for sunbathing.

The central core of the building, which contains the bathrooms, drops down through the old house like an extraneous contemporary insertion, while the existing building conserves its typical characteristics, such as the plaster moldings, paneled carpentry and traditional French windows onto the balconies and the roof terrace.

Different flooring materials and patterns, from herringbone parquet floor, to tongue-and-groove planks, to stone or brick areas for different uses, define and outline the original distribution of the house, often contradicting the new distribution of interior spaces and creating a historical register of the building's earlier state.

The prevalent wall color is white, to reflect as much light as possible, but the areas that are only reached by diffuse indirect illumination are colored orange, creating a series of "hot" insertions that animate the potentially cold atmosphere. This gives certain functions, such as the kitchen cubicle, a separate character, although there is no real or structural segregation from the adjacent dining space.

The building's awkward and unusual volumes, plus the need to leave no storage space unused, required the special design and construction of much of the furniture and cabinetry.

Location:
Torino, Italy
Designteam:
Michele Bonino, Luca Maletto, Stefano Oletto
Contractor:
Make it snc, Torino
Furniture realization:
Marco Masoero, Lessolo
Surface:
100 sqm + 60 sqm terrace
Date design:
December 2004
Start construction:
February 2005
End construction:
October 2005
Building costs:
60.000 €
Photograhs:
Beppe Giardino

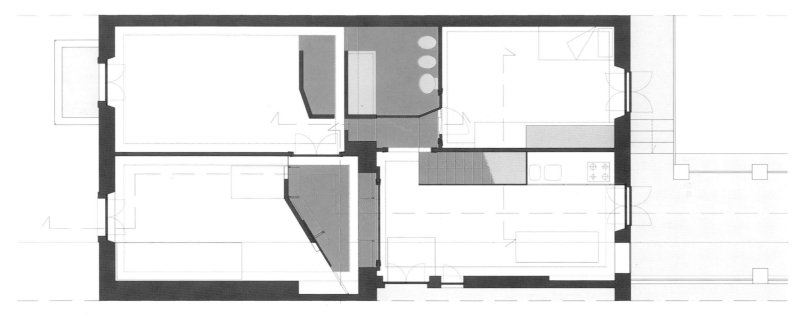

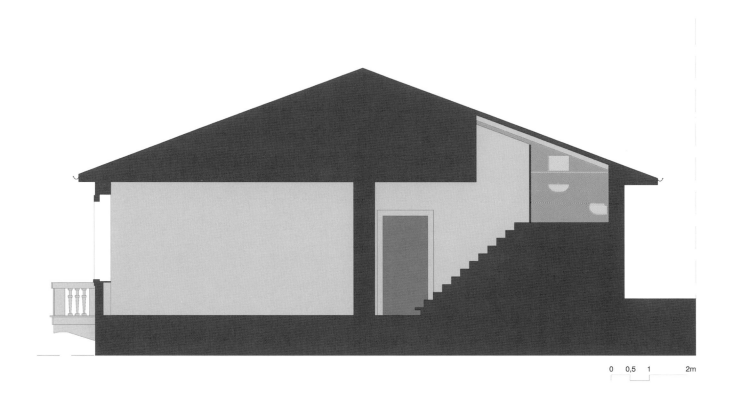

0 0,5 1 2m

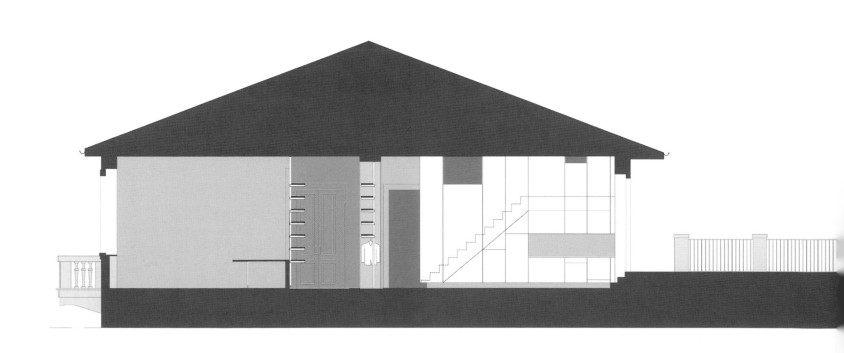

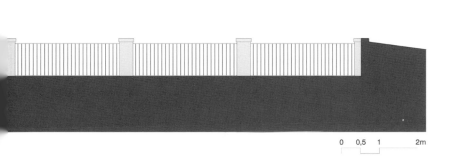

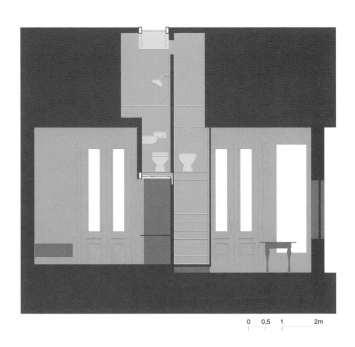

Armand Solà

Loft in Sabadell

The project involved adapting an industrial textile building for use as a family home. The building consisted of two floors of completely uninterrupted space, with considerable heights and large windows facing outside. With these initial characteristics, and given that the lower floor was to maintain its original function, the construction of a mezzanine became the way to use the space under the gabled roof. The dwelling would be organized like a loft, flexibly adaptable to the future requirements of the young couple who were going to inhabit it. Thus, a twofold structural challenge arose: in the first place, the lower chords of the steel roof trusses prevented the upper part of the space from being used; this was solved by transforming the trusses into rigid frames, with angle irons fixed onto each side, so the chord could be cut out without affecting the structure's stability. These angle irons were made unusually heavy, to deal with the second part of the challenge: the mezzanine floor was to be suspended from the roof structure to avoid building pillars through the floors below. Some connections to the previously existing structure were required to avoid any tendency to swing. The first truss in the series was kept as a nostalgic expression of the buildings original state.

The lower floor only contains the entrance hall, with doors through to the workshop on one side or the storage and parking area on the other. The stairs occupy the same place, freed of constricting blind walls.

The main floor is a wide double-height space with a minimal sanitary space to protect the intimacy of the rest of the floor visually, while the brightness of the colors and the numerous elements guessed at are an enticement to proceed.

The distribution of the various zones follows a longitudinal compositional axis that ends at the two large windows overlooking a square. As from here, the only colors are the natural tones of wood, rust, stainless steel and white, there is a constant insistence on visual connections to the upper floor, either through the double height of the living room, or laterally along the longitudinal axis. This connection is reinforced by the windows, the dimensions of which make them serve both floors. The same goes for the radiators, great vertical panels that reinforce a unitary impression.

At the opposite end to the square, the compositional axis terminates at a discreet access to the terrace of the neighboring building, which belongs to the same family. The mezzanine is a wide area for study and work that, in time, can be partitioned into independent bedrooms when needed.

Location:
Sabadell, Barcelona, Spain
Furniture:
Sofa: Perobell
Chairs: Andreu Word
Tables: from the author
Curtains: Cortinova
Photographs:
Eugeni Pons

First floor plan

Ground floor plan

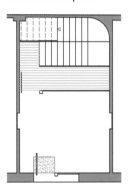

Attic plan

The sobriety of the shapes and the minimalist feeling of its components, in which different materials come together with no transition, the austerity of the colors, all contribute to make this an undeniably beautiful composition. Any domestic item included will establish a contrast, so that in the near future, when the apartment is inhabited, a small intellectual effort will always lead back to the beautiful, serene vision offered by the space in its raw condition.

exe.arquitectura

The Stairway House

The owner of this dwelling required the functional program that is customary concerning the type and number of rooms, with very open, flexible and luminous spaces. The main decision was to get natural light into the dark center of the building, so frequent in floor plans of these dimensions, sandwiched between neighboring party-walls. The resulting project aimed to make the house a generous space through which the inhabitants can flow freely, connecting or separating rooms by means of minimal manipulations.

All of this has been achieved by means of a stairway leading up to a skylight through the roof, with a surface area the size of the entire stairwell. Thus the stairway becomes the dwelling's main feature, functioning as an open center piercing the entire building. Transversally oriented it embodies the vertical communication as well as the horizontal connection and filter, the heart of the dwelling, literally suspended from the central skylight. This stairway distributes the building's other spaces around it, all of which are very open, with the entire volume of the house as the main space. That none of the rooms have doors is made possible by the spatial fluidity, whereby all the separations and filters between areas are achieved by the segmentation of sectors.

Functional differences have been determined according to the use of each space. On the ground floor a double height space gives access to the dwelling and to the garage, creating a cushion space between the street and the building's completely glazed second façade; this extra-tall space and the car become part of the home. Beyond the "second façade", the entire floor is devoid of partitions, only occupied by the stairway, the kitchen, and the dining room area. This is another double height space with a fully glazed façade, faced by the living room space on the floor above. The patio, with a pool at the far end, also becomes part of the home when the French window onto the garden is wide open.

The French window can be completely folded back and there is no interruption in the flooring between indoors and outdoors. The ground floor is a very dynamic space that can absorb multiple situations, becoming the main nucleus of the home.

Half a flight up the stairs is the bathroom, which materializes as a volume suspended from the second façade that opens onto the entrance space. Another half flight up leads to the living-room. This opens onto the double height space of the dining-room and the view outdoors through the two glass façades.

Location:
Molins de Rei, Barcelona, España
Start of construction:
December 2002
Completion of project :
July 2004
Area:
253,20 sqm
Photographs:
Eugeni Pons

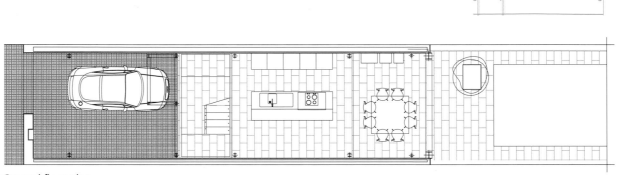

Ground floor plan

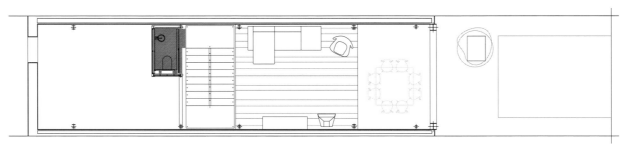

First floor plan

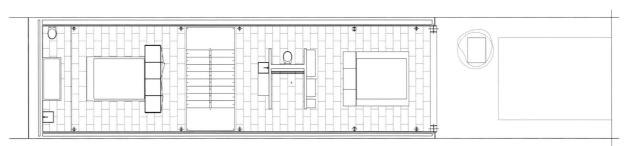

Second floor plan

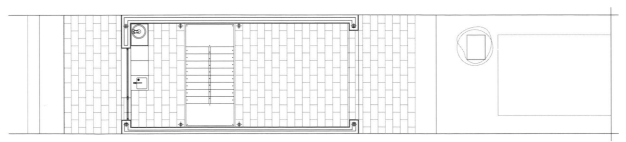

Third floor plan

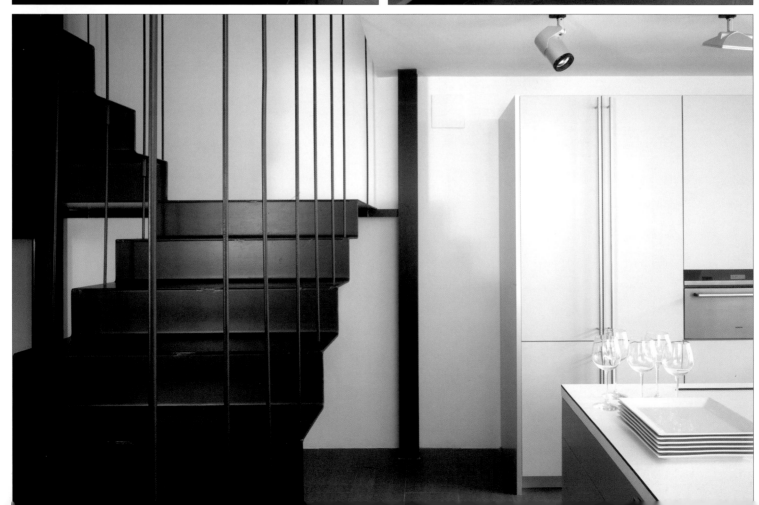

In the floor upstairs there are two bedrooms, only separated by the filter of the tensing cables that sustain the stairs and the volume created by the dwelling's only partitions, those around the master bathroom. The bathroom of the second bedroom is placed directly on the façade and remains open to the room, with a curtain to draw in between if privacy is needed. The studio and the laundry room are on the top floor; both have access to a terrace, one of which is mainly reserved for service and installation purposes, while the studio terrace functions as an outdoor extension of the indoor space.

Messana O'Rorke Architects

The Pent Tank House

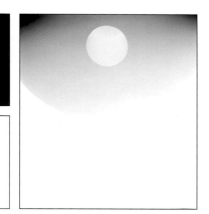

The project involved the renovation of an existing loft apartment and the development of an existing sprinkler tank house into an urban retreat.

The apartment's simple layout was maintained, but reconfigured so that the bedrooms had individual access to a shared bathroom rather than it being accessed from the living space, (a powder room in the entry way meant that guests would not need to access the bathroom). The sky lit bathroom doubled in size and was developed to have a serene spa like quality, with a continuous stone floor, polished waterproof plaster walls, and clear glass shower enclosure. In the living room and bedrooms new storage was introduced at every possible point behind hidden flush lacquer panels. The kitchen was resurfaced and the maple wood floors were lightened and refinished. A custom stainless steel spiral stair replaced an ugly painted steel stair with wood treads. The client anticipated that a new stair would encourage him to ascend more frequently to his roof deck and Tank House.

A tree house perched high in a city of towers and skyscrapers. The tank house was conceived as the quintessential retreat, a room for reading, relaxing and listening to music.

The refurbished roof deck was given new trees and landscape; it had existed for a number of years, over-shadowed by a looming tar covered rotunda occupied by an enormous cast iron sprinkler tank. The removal of this tank and the introduction of a new structural frame to support the crumbling terracotta walls of the rotunda were essential difficulties of this project. The building was shored-up by an external wood frame and the tank was slowly cut into manageable pieces with blowtorches. Once removed the true proportions of the internal space were revealed and it was tempting to leave it as a raw industrial space, but the program requirements and in particular the need for the room to be usable year round meant moving forward as planned.

A twelve-foot tall window was cut into the east side of the space and the new window looked out onto the roof deck plantings. A circular skylight was introduced into center, casting an ethereal light into the space. The floor of maple matched the apartment and was segmented into removable panels providing access to storage space below.

Location:
New York, USA
Photographs:
Elizabeth Felicella

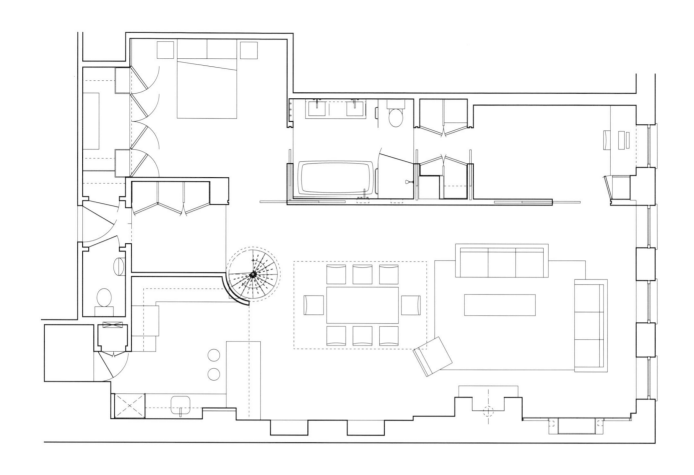

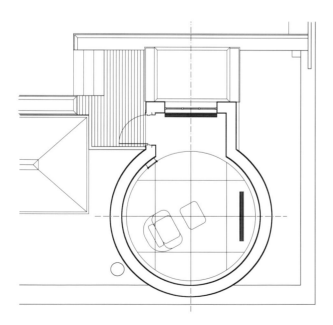

The sky lit bathroom doubled in size and was developed to have a serene spa like quality, with a continuous stone floor, polished waterproof plaster walls, and clear glass shower enclosure. In the living room and bedrooms new storage was introduced at every possible point behind hidden flush lacquer panels.

Eduard Samsó

Duplex apartment in Sarrià

This attractive town house is in the desirable location of Sarrià, an uptown neighborhood in Barcelona. The ground floor covers an area of 120 sqm while the first floor is an expansive 270 sqm. Both floors were formerly dedicated to office space.

At street level the entrance gives on to a small hallway which leads to the kitchen, dining room and a sitting room-cum-study which is raised a few centimeters and affords glimpses of the garden. A staircase to the sleeping area leads from here, making various turns to get to the top. On this next level are three particularly large bedrooms and two bathrooms. In the kitchen a wall made of cupboards hides the utility area and a spare cloakroom for guests.

Returning to the entrance hall, there is a side staircase which runs parallel to a curved wooden wall and leads to the living room on the upper floor. This room has various different areas where you can relax and chat, watch films or television, or read and work in the adjoining studio. It gives on to a balcony which looks over the garden and the property's swimming pool. The sleeping quarters are reached through a side door which gives on to a short corridor. This passageway houses a cloakroom, the door to the garden and to the garage.

As there was little available height, false ceilings to hide and distribute the air conditioning ducts and lighting wires had to be built of shallow tongue-and-groove wood paneling.

In the loft there is a combination of white walls with solid oak parquet flooring and travertine in the wet area. These subtle and natural contrasts provide a perfect backdrop for a hand-picked selection of chairs, ranging from modern classics to other more avant-garde pieces. In the kitchen the wooden floor, cupboards and roof contrast strikingly with the cool stainless steel of the work station and the electrical appliances.

Location:
Barcelona, Spain
Photographs:
Jordi Miralles

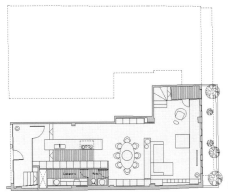

Ground floor plan

First floor plan

Lazzarini Pickering Architects

Apartment in Montecarlo

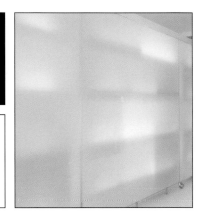

On the 14th floor of the Mirabeau building, two apartments have been made into one, occupying 95 sqm plus 30 sqm of terrace. The client spends several days a week in Montecarlo. He lives alone and usually eats out. Like a first class suite on a liner, the apartment is perfect for breakfast and aperitifs at sunset. The project interprets the wish of the client for a single, continuous, fluid space.

The concrete bearing wall that divides the apartment longitudinally is dematerialized by mirrors, glass volumes that seem to pass from one side to the other, and portals in stainless steel. The bathrooms, kitchen and wardrobes are pure volumes inserted into the single space. The terrace, conceived as part of the interior, expands it and provides fluidity.

The three-dimensional fronts of the volumes pivot on stainless steel rods. The luminous shelves are cantilevered from the wall. Colored cinema filters on the luminous shelves create infinite chromatic configurations. The pivoting panels (including the opaque ones) are designed to be left open. Conceived as rotating volumes, they create different perspectives in a dynamic space.

As it turns, the large door/mirror that divides the living area from the bedroom alters the perception of space, in a virtual play of reflections. Doubling the perspectives, it multiplies the terrace, bringing the sea and sky indoors.

The bathroom extends the bedroom. The shower is behind the bed and the glass division makes it possible to shower watching the sea. Shiny surfaces, transparent glass and backlit volumes, mirror the sources of artificial light and capture the light of day. The glass volume on the terrace changes color as the day passes, as the internal volumes do with artificial light. Metallic in the morning, it becomes a natural lamp as the sun moves behind in the afternoon.

In the living space the sofa is "Magister" by Antonio Citterio for Flexform, the tables are 'Servente' by Lazzarini-Pickering for Acierno ISL. The two chairs are original Louis XV. The bed is 'Dormusa' by Lazzarini-Pickering for Acierno ISL. The spotlights are by Kreon.

Location:
Monaco, Montecarlo
Site coordinator:
Antonio Ferretti
Realisation:
ARBET s.r.l.
Photographs:
Matteo Piazza

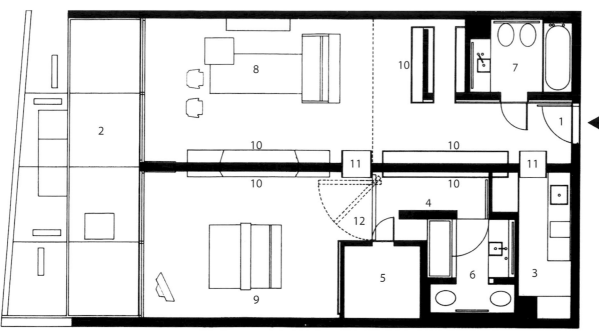

1. Entrance
2. Loggia
3. Kitchen
4. Lumber-room
5. Shower
6. Bathroom
7. Guest bathroom
8. Living room
9. Bedroom
10. Glass cabinet
11. Steel doorway
12. Mirror doorway

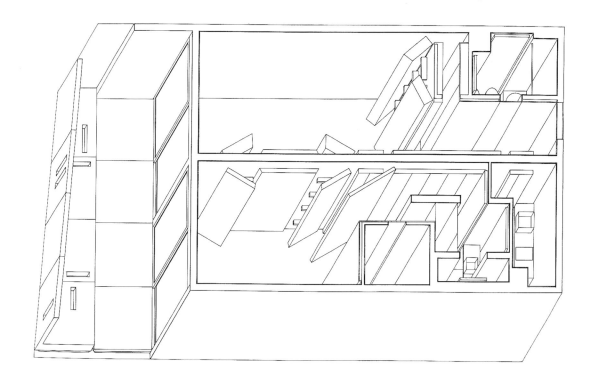

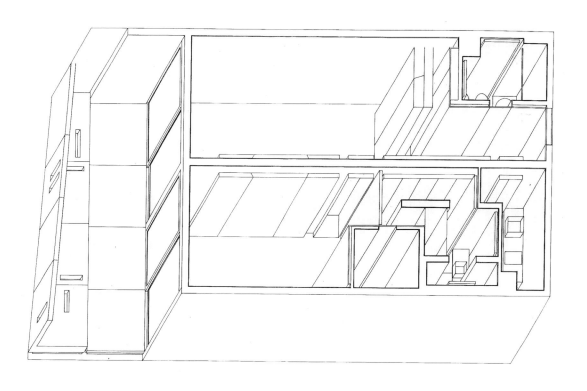

Filippo Bombace

Laura House

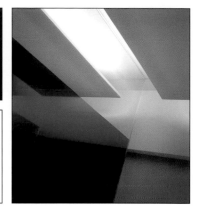

Uncompromising lines and 90° angles are the predominant feature of this Roman apartment for a young professional woman. Counterpoint rules the distribution, with a daring juxtaposition of the kitchen-pantry and a shower, visually open both to the pantry and to the dining room-lounge. Their form and position define these two areas as the dwelling's central core.

The openings are oriented along the north-south axis. The entrance hall is small but balanced, separated from the other rooms by a sheet of frosted glass; the living room has a corner sofa opposite the TV wall, with a custom-made, white lacquered shelf. The dining room's main feature is the special design of the table, with a sheet of glass on white –lacquered legs; the piece is symmetrically illuminated by spotlights embedded in the floor and the ceiling. The strictly minimalist pantry is made of MK, clad in glossy-white lacquered panels and stainless steel worktops. The appliances, plumbing fixtures and Neff hood are perfectly integrated into the impeccable plasterboard surfaces. The studio has been housed behind the kitchen, where it can be partly closed off by means of a sliding panel of dark oak.

The shower-fountain is the central focus of the apartment, with a stone basin holding a layer of loose river pebbles; only the shower fixture emerges from the ceiling, which houses the embedded lights. There is also a small guest bathroom.

Parallel to the studio is the mini bedroom suite, with a white lacquered cupboard and a bed placed under another custom-made cupboard. The main bathroom, partly clad in glossy grey tiles, has a great shower space between a sheet of clear glass and a window, protected by a waterproof curtain. The basin rests on a dark oak-wood top that stands out against the cloud-blue wall.

The atmosphere is ruled by bluish lighting reflected by the pure white forms of the furniture and the walls. Only the bedroom allows a warmer hue, where the white light does not alter the basic color of the walls and the ceiling. The floors are paved in wengé wood. The lighting system combines halogen spotlights and fluorescent tubes, making the elegant atmosphere intriguing and variable.

Location:
Roma, Italy
Collaborators:
Federico Battistoni
Valentina Brindisi
Photographs:
Luigi Filetici

1. Entrance
2. Living room
3. Kitchen
4. Studio
5. Shower
6. Guest bathroom
7. Bedroom
8. Master bathroom
9. Balcony

0   1 m   2m

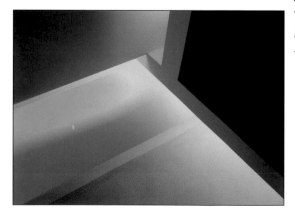

The atmosphere is ruled by bluish lighting reflected by the pure white forms of the furniture and the walls. Only the bedroom allows a warmer hue, where the white light does not alter the basic color of the walls and the ceiling.

The floors are paved in wengé wood. The lighting system combines halogen spotlights and fluorescent tubes, making the elegant atmosphere intriguing and variable.

Ángel Valdés

House in Palafolls

This house is located in the small town of Palafolls, in the Maresme, a coastal region north of Barcelona, about an hour away from the city. The project originated from a need to extend a home which was part of an established building set out as a ground floor, first floor and attic.

The extension involved adding a second floor, reached from a communal access, a hallway and by a lift which had to be newly installed.

Access to the home is made either by using the communal staircase or the lift which goes to the second floor: at this level there is an entrance hall, a fully equipped bathroom, three bedrooms, a kitchen and a sitting room. In addition a terrace runs around the side of the building.

The daytime areas are oriented towards the terrace, while the night time spaces give on to the rear façade. The interior design has a strong contemporary feel with the predominance of straight lines and cubic volumes running throughout the space. This is a wonderfully luminous home enhanced by the pure white of both walls and furniture. In turn they form a dramatic contrast with the black elements resulting in a two-tone look which is strikingly austere yet at the same timer remarkably comfortable. Only the Panton chairs, also in white, add a suggestion of curvaceous lines to the otherwise straight angles of the furniture. The floor in the living area is one of the few concessions to warmth, a carefully chosen parquet in attractive light tones.

The kitchen is totally cutting edge: all the services are neatly together down one wall. This utility area is complemented by a central island work space, which has been elongated to serve as a dining table. The cooker hood is a distinctive feature in this space, dropping directly out of the ceiling: a cylindrical form made out of stainless steel which in this central point contrasts well with the straight lines that characterize the rest of the home.

A private staircase leads up to the attic area. This comprises an entrance hall, a bedroom with its own walk-in dressing room and a fully equipped bathroom. There is also another terrace at this level. The attic's ceiling is formed by the building's sloping roof and measures 27m². The overall lines of clean and orthogonal angles together with the contrasting black and white colors is repeated on this floor, echoing the style of the main living area below. The sloping roof combined with the outstanding luminosity give added value to the volumetric concept of the space. The living area on the main floor can also enjoy this great sense of space and light thanks to its generous double height.

Location:
Palafolls, Girona, España
Area:
124,20 sqm
Photographs:
José Luis Hausmann

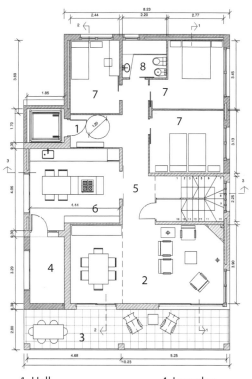
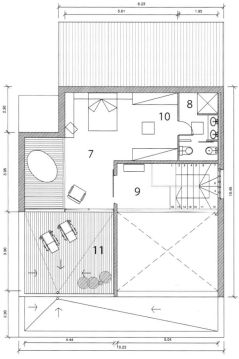
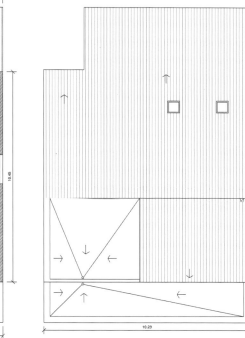

1. Hall

2. Dining - living room

3. Gallery

4. Laundry

5. Corridor

6. Kitchen

7. Bedroom

8. Bathroom

9. Staircase hall

10. Dressing room

11. Terrace

Side elevation

Side elevation

Front elevation

Back elevation

Section 1-1

Section 2-2

Section 3-3

David Mikhail Architects

St. Cyr Helen

Faced with the daunting limitations of two dark garages in a cramped site in a classical Georgian mews in London, architect David Mikhail has managed to create an exciting contemporary house full of light and space, minimal yet warm, answering the clients' needs to combine business and home under one roof. Despite its bold frontage the house sits discreetly amidst its more traditional Kensington neighbors being the same height and curiously thanks to a slight bend in the road.

A key to its transformation was the positioning of windows to maximize available light: the double-height glass at the front and a long rood window at the rear as well as a small shaft that also creates a small courtyard. Space was gained by dropping the ground floor to below pavement level, a technique frequently used in London, allowing room for a third level at the top of the house and yet staying within the limits of scale that the neighboring buildings impose.

The bedrooms and bathrooms are on the ground floor, turning the usual order of London houses around. One bedroom has a view out to the small pebbled courtyard with a mere touch of greenery, designed for the minimum of maintenance and the maximum tranquility and privacy.

The first floor combines the different functions of cooking, eating and relaxation, and is physically as well as practically at the centre of the organization of the spaces in the house. Folding glass panels, like those in the bedroom, lead the kitchen out to a small terrace.

The top mezzanine level provides extra work space and emphasizes the sense of height from the central living space. The shape of the steel joists in the living room is just one example of the angularity inherent in much of the design, part of a style in which structure is the predominant feature, and whose geometrical form is echoed in and complemented by such features as the girder-like construction of the Le Corbusier dining table.

The house is also fired up by solid planes of brilliant color on the walls and set off further by the vivid coloring and organic shapes of modern furniture design like the mauve and blue Pierre Paulin bucket chairs which, while softening the effect through their rich fabric and subtle curves, bring about a sense of unity between the house structure and its furnishings as do the wire dining chairs by Warren Platner from 1966 reflecting the sculptural shapes of furniture from the 50s and 60s. The kitchen area is clearly defined with a strong yellow and its own light source through sandblasted glass.

Angles and planes, glass and metal, the warmth of wood and bold colors, all combine to make a light, bright contemporary mix in this modern mews. Although the sparse character of minimalism has had a pervading influence on the design of recent years, the comfortable functionality of such houses as this would seem to be a more practical and welcoming solution for those who want structure, style and the space in which to enjoy it.

Location:
London, UK
Photographs:
Henry Wilson/Redcover.com

The first floor combines the different functions of cooking, eating and relaxation, and is physically as well as practically at the centre of the organization of the spaces in the house. Folding glass panels, like those in the bedroom, lead the kitchen out to a small terrace. The kitchen area is clearly defined with a strong yellow and its own light source through sandblasted glass.

Manel Torres (IN Decoración)

Loft in an old factory

This compact 70 sqm loft is located in one corner of an old factory which continues working today as an industrial warehouse to store building materials. One end of the building was refurbished to create this home which is cut off from the day to day business of the warehouse, having its own entrance which gives directly on to the street.

The refurbishment has produced a result which is a far cry from the original use of this building: what was an old factory is now a young, dynamic space where day to day living is made easy and comfortable, two basic requirements for today's pace of life.

As the given space is quite narrow it was decided from the start to arrange an obstacle-free distribution, so the kitchen and dining room become one unique space, resolved according to the color scheme in the dining room area. This stems predominantly from the circular rug in which the black background acts as a base for a series of smaller circles laid out in concentric rings of different colors. These colors lead the color scheme of the different objects in the room.

In the center of the space is the dining room, consisting of a rugged-looking wenge stained oak table with straight geometric lines and surrounded by four chairs upholstered in red. This merges with the kitchen where the work surface is laid out in an L-shape, convenient for serving guests at the dining table as well as organizing the flow through the apartment.

The bedroom and the bathroom are the only rooms hidden from sight. The bedroom is situated on a mezzanine floor which was built in the ample space provided by the height of the loft. A staircase constructed on one of the side walls leads up to this area; its open stairs don't break up the visual flow through the space. The attic-like ceiling in the bedroom lends it a warm, intimate feel. The low-lying bed fills the centre of the mezzanine on an oak base.

The mezzanine itself is made of pine which has been stained walnut color and its design is simple and straightforward: the low bed in the middle, a wardrobe and strong, brightly colored bed coverings, echoing the style of the main floor below.

The bathroom is tucked in behind the kitchen. Here it was decided to introduce a slightly rustic feel, with a terracotta flooring, exposed beams and a sponged treatment in earthy tones on the walls . The state-of-the-art bathroom fittings provide the perfect contrast with their innovative modern lines.

This modern refurbishment has a young person's style, dynamic and unbuttoned. It has no pretensions but on the contrary is all about making life easier and providing its users with a space that satisfies their needs and provides all the necessary services.

Location:
Palau de Plegamans, Spain
Photographs:
José Luis Hausmann

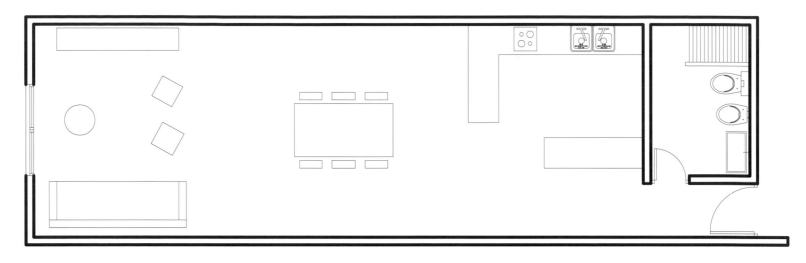

Voon Wong & VX designs

Apartment in Manchester Street

A home in the heart of London's West End is a privilege and a luxury envied by many and achieved by very few. And when it's located in Manchester Street, within the confines of the historic Portman Estate, allowing you to walk to work, the theatre, Regent's Park or Soho restaurants then it's beyond most people's dreams. However the client who commissioned Voon Wong to design this home conversion lives that dream, and what's more towers over the rest of the neighborhood from his lofty height on top of a 1960s office and residential block. Not only does he live about as central as you can get, but also in a home flooded with light and endlessly fascinating views.

Singapore-born architect Voon Wong, tipped as a talent to watch, was briefed to create a comfortable living space, incorporating a home office, on the top floor of an uncompromising 60s block. The work involved radically demolishing the original interior of the eighth floor and reconfiguring the accommodation to create a kitchen, two bedrooms and bathrooms and a large living/dining area.

One of the key challenges was to bring light and texture from the perimeter of the building to the centre of the apartment which according to the architect was achieved by using "a rich palette of materials". In the case of an interior bathroom for example the clean lines of the fittings, pale tones, textures and mirrored wall all serve to bounce the light which passes through a translucent wall, making it a bright, luminous space.

There is a minimalist uncluttered feel about furniture and fittings with clean lines and angles, slight texture in wall coverings and panels of color. The London based architect still shows clear signs of his oriental origins.

The central focus of the apartment is the spectacular spiral staircase which leads up to the office on the roof. Positioned on a wooden plinth it seems to swirl up into the infinite light above, a sculpture of steel and air, solid yet ethereal. It emerges in the midst of the glass box, an artwork itself.

This glass pavilion is raised slightly above the ninth floor roof terrace with wooden steps leading down to the wonderful landscaped area with its decking, loungers and shrubbery. The pavilion's full-height glass panels offer panoramic views across the roofscapes of central London. Materials used in the glass pavilion were more restrained than in the living area to complement the rich vistas that surround it. There is little that can detract from such magnificent views but the simplicity of the glass box is beauty itself and the crowning glory to this impressive conversion.

Location:
London, UK
Area:
200 sqm
Client:
Derek Butler
Structural Engineers:
Elliott Wood Partnership
Electrical & Mechanical Engineers:
Fulcrum Consulting
Main Contractors:
Claremont Construction
Photographs:
Henry Wilson/Redcover.com

BOCA RATON PUBLIC LIBRARY, FLORIDA

3 3656 0451837 4

747.88314 Bro
Broto, Carles.
Apartment interiors /